TEDDY BEARS AT SCHOOL

An Activities Handbook For Teachers of Young Children

Arleen Steen, Ph.D., and Martha L. Lane

Illustrations adapted by Nancy Lane Feldner

Humanics Limited
Atlanta, Georgia

Humanics Limited
A Gary B. Wilson Company
P.O. Box 7447
Atlanta, Georgia 30309
(404) 874-2176

*Dedicated to joy and self-confidence
in the Early Childhood classrooms.*

Especially for

Bethany

Katie

David

About the Authors

Arleen Steen and Marty Lane have worked on behalf of young children throughout their careers totaling more than fifty years.

Dr. Steen works with undergraduate and graduate students at Miami University in Oxford, Ohio. She teaches courses in Early Childhood Education and Language Arts. After completing her doctorate at the University of Iowa in 1969, she taught kindergarten at McGuffey Laboratory School, Miami University, for seven years. She also worked with young children, ages four to eight, in Cedar Rapids, Iowa, where she grew up. She enjoys needlework, crafts, houseplants, and Sirikit, her Siamese cat.

Mrs. Lane teaches kindergarten in the Trotwood-Madison District, near Dayton, Ohio, where she also taught and directed Head Start. Mrs. Lane earned her master's degree in Early Childhood Education in 1974 at Wright State University in Dayton, Ohio, her home town. She thoroughly enjoys her free time with her daughter and her family. She is an avid reader and gardens with the help of her dog, Megan.

Dr. Steen and Mrs. Lane have worked together since 1971 on a variety of projects including many original games for kindergarteners. For the past ten years, Mrs. Lane has served as a consultant for the Early Childhood workshops that Dr. Steen has directed at Miami University.

Both Dr. Steen and Mrs. Lane have become archtophiles (Teddy Bear lovers) and avid collectors as a result of the children's contagious enthusiastic response to the Teddy Bear Centers. They hope you will enjoy Teddy Bears, too.

Acknowledgments

We wish to thank the many teachers in southwest Ohio who have bravely experimented with our first bear games and activities, especially Betsy Z. Lavelle and Susan S. Portman.

We wish to thank the many college students who were so encouraging as the book began to take shape. We thank those who constructed games from our first plans and made suggestions to make the book better. Our thanks especially to Amy Hill, Linda Nellesson, and Lisa Mills.

And to Marcia Burchfield, a bear maker beyond compare, we owe a special thanks for her unique contributions.

And to our families, for their patience and support in this whole "bear" venture.

Contents

Chapter One

INTRODUCTION
TO TEDDY BEARS

Teddy Bears Are For Hugging! How Did They Get to School?

Each year we worked hard to arrange our kindergarten rooms so that they were practical, attractive, and appealing to the new students. As we arranged centers, we gave our Book Corners special attention to attract the children to them. We filled the corners with many colorfully illustrated, well written, fascinating books, both familiar and new. Rather than randomly selecting books, occasionally we chose books on a particular theme. An obvious choice was bear books because the selection was almost unlimited.

After arranging a Teddy Bear Book Corner for the first few weeks of school, we were delighted with the response. The children were drawn to this center. The conversations about their own experiences with Teddy Bears prompted us to include real Teddy Bears to encourage additional interaction. Because the children were so interested, more Teddy Bears, bear games, and activities were added. Puzzles, games, and costumes for dramatizations were enthusiastically welcomed by the children. One commercial activity, Milton Bradley's Teddy Bear Counters, was particularly fascinating, and the children used it in many different ways.

As each new kindergarten year began, what worked so well before was repeated, with variations. The foundation for the Teddy Bear Center was always books. Each year additional items were added to the Teddy Bear Corner. Children brought in a wide assortment of bears to share, and the annual Teddy Bear parade began. New Teddy Bears and bear-related activities appeared on the commercial market. Many found homes and hugs in our classroom.

The children responded wholeheartedly to the new bear activities and were thoroughly involved in the Teddy Bear Center. As we realized that all of the children's needs could not be met with the available commercial materials, the next logical step was to design bear games and activities that helped us meet our curriculum goals and objectives. *Teddy Bears at School* is the result of that effort.

All of the materials have been tried in our classrooms. The children have spontaneously offered their evaluations. Many teachers have experimented with the Teddy Bear games and loved them, too.

Why Should Teddy Bears Be at School?

Teddy Bears Are:

Familiar. Teddy Bears are a familiar toy to most young children. When children enter a new school situation and find a Teddy Bear, school is less threatening. The children immediately feel more comfortable and are willing to explore their new environment.

Friendly. Most children find Teddy Bears good companions. This friendly atmosphere gives the children a sense of well-being and an eagerness to explore bear-related learning activities.

Different. There is probably a wider variety of bears available than any other single toy. That very diversity allows for an abundance of early childhood activities including: ordering, classifying, comparing, and developing and using descriptive language.

Easy to talk to. Because Teddy Bears are so acceptable, children often have conversations with bears and tell stories about bears. This interaction helps develop beginning language skills.

13

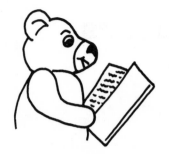

Found in books. For a long time there has been an abundance of children's books using bears as central characters. In addition to offering literary merit, this rich source can be used as the foundation for a variety of experiences including listening skills, language development, and dramatization.

Visually appealing. Plastic and stuffed bears, books, games, stickers, erasers, mugs, towels, and soaps are just some of the almost unending variety of bears appearing in the world of commercial products for children. This commercial diversity encourages children to accept their own artistic attempts and explore many media.

Abundant. Most early childhood classrooms already have many commercial bear materials including puppets, felt board stories, songs, and games. When these activities are together and spotlighted early in the year, the children are more likely to adjust smoothly and adapt quickly to academic material.

Playful. When children immerse themselves in play with Teddy Bears, independence and self-confidence evolve. This independent and sure attitude is then brought to the Teddy Bear Center.

Teddy Bears at school? Of course!

How to Use This Book

Teddy Bears at School is divided into seven chapters: Introduction to Bears, Introduction to Centers, Language Arts Activities, Mathematics Activities, Motor Activities, Teddy Bear Week, and Self-concept Unit. The introduction to centers chapter offers alternatives in setting up a classroom and scheduling for young children. Managing learning centers and personalizing learning are emphasized.

The next three chapters present a wide assortment of bear activities: Chapter 3, Language Arts; Chapter 4, Mathematics; and Chapter 5, Motor Skills. Each activity includes a title, an objective, a list of materials, construction information, and directions for using the activity in the classroom. Many alternatives are given for teaching basic concepts.

Chapter 6 shows how selected activities from *Teddy Bears At School* can be used to improve self-concept.

The final chapter, Teddy Bear Week, describes a variety of activities that can celebrate Teddy Bears.

A successful center need not contain all the activities in this book. Large group literature activities are included because they draw children to the center's bear books.

INTRODUCTION TO CENTERS

Developing
A Learning Center

What is a center?

1. A center is a place where children work independently or in small groups with an organized set of materials.
2. A center can be:
   a. one activity or many activities.
   b. a single concept or several concepts grouped under a single topic.
   c. as small as a shoebox (magnetic letters).
   d. as big as one-fourth of a room (blocks).

What is the purpose of a center?

1. The main purpose of a center is to meet curriculum objectives.
   a. The objectives should be chosen in accordance with district curriculum goals.
   b. Objectives should be appropriate to student levels. There is no need to build a center with objectives already mastered by the majority of the class.
   c. Center objectives should be those which can best be met by activities and games that are designed to be used by individuals or small groups.
   d. Not all school goals and objectives can be met in centers.
2. Centers encourage children to develop independence.
3. Centers allow for a variety of small group activities by providing an enjoyable alternative to whole group instruction.
4. By stimulating interests and giving children a choice, centers allow for different learning styles and different learning levels.

How are activities selected for a center?

1. Before designing a center, the teacher must think about the unique characteristics of individual students and the class as a whole. The teacher must consider that students have varying levels of:
   a. competencies.
      1) How much does each child know about the subject in the center?
      2) How much does each child know about the materials in the center?

   b. independence in work habits.
   c. social development.

18

2. Selections should include activities which offer a choice. They should:
   a. range from very easy to challenging.
   b. provide for varying attention spans.
   c. promote review and reinforcement.
   d. satisfy and be fun to do.
   e. provide for individual and small group participation.
   f. provide for different learning modes: auditory, visual, kinesthetic.
   g. include independent and parallel activities.
3. When selecting activities:
   a. choose materials that reinforce rather than introduce a new concept.
   b. use simple games with clear directions.
   c. use games and activities with familiar formats.
      1) Dominoes
      2) Puzzles
      3) Concentration
   d. use or adapt some commercial games.
      1) Candyland
      2) Old Maid
   e. choose only an adequate number of games.
      1) Take away those games not used.
      2) Remove unused or seldom used games and re-introduce at a later date (perhaps with modification).
      3) Keep the center "alive" by new additions.
   f. illustrate directions for beginning readers.
   g. be prepared for student rejection of some activities.
4. Not all activities related to a specific objective necessarily work in a center. Complex activities or some of those requiring gross motor movement should take place outside the center.

What attracts children to centers?

A special, intriguing item can be the reason to develop a center on a particular theme. Fascinating objects may be used in a center to provide atmosphere or develop interest. These attention getters must not interfere with the primary purpose of a center. Below is a list of attention getters.
1. Fascinating items which so strongly appeal to the child that they draw him into the activities at the center:
   - Favorite book
   - Classroom pet
   - Stuffed toy
   - Adult tool
   - Article of clothing (hat)
   - Picture
   - Miniatures
   - Toys
     - Unique object brought by child or parent

19

2. Fragile "untouchables" may be included, but items which children cannot handle should be kept to a minimum. Some examples are:
   - Antiques
   - Delicate flower arrangements
   - Anything made of glass
3. Unique arrangements which encourage participation and/or dramatic play such as:
   - Round objects and games on round table
   - Red objects and games on red shelves
   - Games on bulletin board
   - Walk-ins (restaurant, supermarket, library, cave, doctor's office, house, three bears' cottage, and so on).
4. Interesting neighborhood happenings which can lead to follow-up activities in the classroom. Some examples are:
   - Building a road
   - Street cleaning
   - Building construction
   - Phone lineman working
   - Passing fire truck or emergency vehicle

How does the teacher choose a center title?

1. Each center needs a title to establish its identity. The titles should be:
   a. short and easy to identify. *Bear*, rather than *Big Brave Brown Bear's Bench*.
   b. general enough to allow for many activities. *Bear*, rather than *Bear's Writing Table*.
   c. easy to code so that games can be readily identified. *Bear*, rather than *Imagination*.
2. Avoid cutesy or bizarre titles that encourage misbehavior, such as *The Silly Six Center*.

Managing a Center

How does the teacher introduce a center?

1. Children may explore freely the activities in a given center.
2. The teacher may introduce center activities one at a time.
   a. Difficult activities should be introduced to small groups.
   b. Activities with simple formats such as puzzles may be introduced to the whole class.

When do students use centers?

About one-third of the students' school day should be spent in self-directed activities.

1. The teacher may establish a time when all students use centers.
   a. All children may choose from all available centers such as: Bear Center, Blocks, Red Center, Housekeeping, Sand Play.
   b. All children may choose from available centers in one subject such as art: paint, crayons, clay, cut and paste, markers.
2. The teacher may establish a time when small groups of students use centers. Some students may use centers while the teacher works with a small group.
3. Students may visit centers after finishing other assignments.

Which activities will students do?

1. Students may choose from all activities.
2. Students do activities only at their level.
3. Students are required to do every activity.
4. Students are required to complete any one activity.
5. Students complete assigned center activity.
   a. All students complete a given activity.
   b. Selected students who need a skill complete an activity.

How does the teacher control the number of students in a center?

1. Students tell the teacher where they want to go. The teacher limits the number of children in a center by granting or refusing requests.
2. Students place their name tags in the pocket chart next to the preferred center. When the pocket chart is full, so is the center.
3. The teacher provides space and materials for a limited number of students in each center, such as providing four balls of clay for four students.
4. The teacher provides related items or tags such as bears for the bear center, aprons for the restaurant or keys to the house center.

How do the teacher and children care for materials in the center?

1. The teacher plans storage as the center is planned.
   a. Organizes games and activities so that similar ones are together on the shelves.
   b. Designates a specific place in the center for project materials such as crayons and scissors.
   c. Codes game boxes for return to specific shelves.
      1) Store red boxes on the red shelf.
      2) Number games and activities for return to the Math Center.
2. The teacher works with the children to develop the skills necessary for care of the materials.

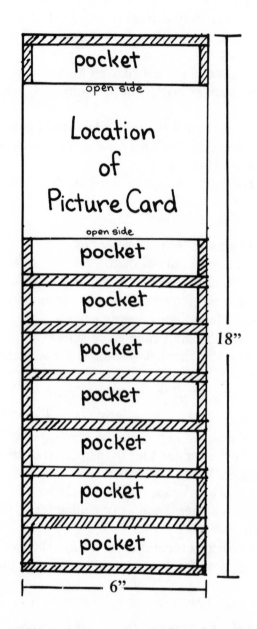

pocket

open side

Location
of
Picture Card

open side

pocket

pocket

pocket

pocket

pocket

pocket

pocket

18"

6"

How does the teacher help the children feel comfortable with center activity?

1. The classroom atmosphere must be such that the child feels free to make responsible use of materials, activities, and suggestions.
2. Because children are expected to use centers independently, time for exploration must be allowed and mistakes must be accepted as learning experiences.
3. General classroom rules concerning noise level, movement,

sharing, respecting the rights of others, and care of equipment should be consistent with learning center rules.

When should a center be developed?

Consider developing a center:

    a. when curriculum objectives can best be met in an individual or small group situation.

    b. when some children have a special interest in a topic or a special need for review or reinforcement.

    c. when available materials need to be organized for efficiency and accountability.

    d. when materials need to be arranged to stimulate interest in a new topic or unit.

    e. when developing an enjoyable atmosphere by organizing activities within an interesting theme (Teddy Bear).

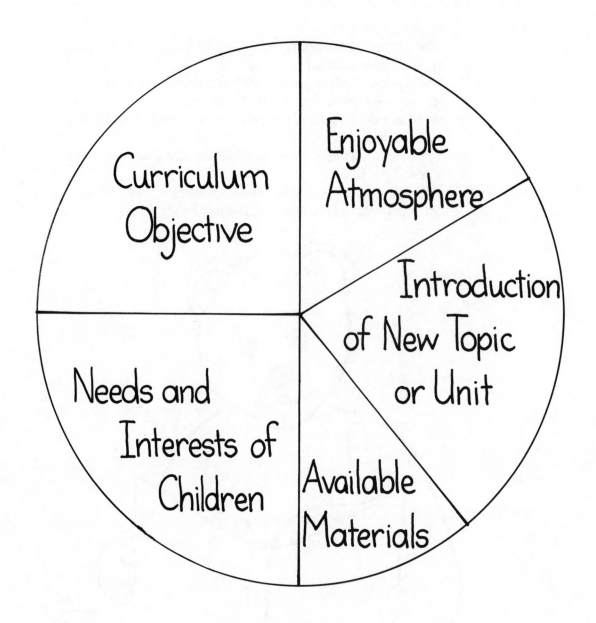

Center Considerations

What is accountability?

1. Accountability is a record of a child's progress toward completion of a given task.
2. Accountability is not an evaluation of the success of the child.

How can the teacher organize tasks to help children be accountable?

1. Color coding. Teacher color codes all activities by objectives. Child completes a blue game, a game in blue box or a game with a blue dot.
2. Arrangement of materials. Teacher arranges materials in the center. For example: Child completes tasks in order assigned. First complete the bear puzzle, then make a clay bear.
3. Design of materials. Teacher designs materials which yield a finished product. Product can be shown to the teacher, displayed on the bulletin board, or brought to group time. Products might be a finished puppet or dot-to-dot page.
4. Task cards. Teacher constructs task card describing each activity. Child selects or is assigned one task card. After completing the task, child returns the task card to the teacher (or a box). (See Task Card Development, Chapter 2).
5. Numbered lists. Teacher numbers all the center activities. Teacher distributes or posts a numbered list. Child completes activities 2, 4 and 5 on the numbered bear list.

How can accountability records be kept?

1. The child may keep a record of completed activities by:
   a. coloring in a square.
   b. coloring in a figure.
   c. placing finished product on a bulletin board.
   d. checking off activities on a list.
   e. crossing names off a list.
   f. adding names to a list.
   g. bringing his finished product to group time.
   h. telling another child how to play a game.
2. The teacher may choose to keep track of each child's completed tasks. Teachers, volunteers, or older students can keep records by:
   a. checking names off a list.
   b. listening to child describe activity.
   c. giving reward when task is completed.
      1) stickers
      2) sticker dots
      3) certificates
      4) preparing individual graphs

d. tape recording child's response
   1) Use a picture book to retell a story to recorder.
   2) Describe steps in an art project.

What is evaluation?

1. Evaluation is how successfully the child meets the objectives.
2. Evaluation is more than accountability; it is necessary to analyze the quality of the child's work.

How does the teacher evaluate the child's progress?

1. The teacher reviews the center's objectives.
2. The teacher analyzes the child's work as it relates to center objectives.
3. If the child meets the center's objectives, he may:
   a. be assigned to another center.
   b. return to the same center for reinforcement.
4. If the child does not meet the center's objectives he may:
   a. need specific teacher help in understanding the concepts or skills required to meet the objective.
   b. return to the same center with a specific assignment.
   c. be assigned to another center.

How does the teacher evaluate the success of the center?

1. A successful center must:
   a. help children meet the given objectives.
   b. help children develop independent work habits.
   c. provide joy in learning.
   d. be voluntarily used by many children.
2. If a center is not successful, the teacher should consider:
   a. asking the children for suggestions.
   b. modifying some of the existing activities.
   c. adding or removing activities.
   d. meeting objectives through large group activities.

Creating and Constructing Center Games and Activities

Although this book is not intended to answer all questions concerning game and activity construction, the following ideas and information will help you be more successful.

Included in this section are suggestions on the following:

Contact Pockets   Lettering

Durability   Task Card Development

Familiar Formats   Paper Cutting Tools

Felt Pens   Paper Products

Felt Boards   Self-Checking

Game Boards   Sticky Stuff

Illustrations and Labels   Storage

Move Indicators and Playing Pieces

Contact Pockets

Custom contact pockets are very useful for
- holding cards for a game
- holding titles for storage boxes
- mini-pocket chart.

POCKET DIRECTIONS for 3-inch by 5-inch cards

Directions which follow are for pockets on the Mini-Pocket Chart. The large pocket at the top can hold the picture name card for the center, the small pockets are name tags.

MATERIALS for mini-pocket chart

- Contact: 14 inches by 18 inches
- oak tag: 6 inches by 18 inches
- index cards — 3-inch by 5-inch, cut in half, for name tags
- index cards — 5-inch by 8-inch for pictures
- Scotch Magic Tape (¾ inch)

CONSTRUCTION for Pocket Chart

1. Cut eight pieces of clear Contact, 3½ inches by 8 inches.
2. Outline pattern shown on Contact.
3. Peel off backing.
4. Fold upper half of Contact (smaller piece) on top of the lower piece. This leaves the sticky edge around three sides of the pocket.
5. Mount the first pocket on the top edge of the oak tag, so the open edge of the pocket points down. Fold the pocket edges around the top and sides. Clip the excess at the corners. (This pocket holds the top edge of the picture card).
6. Mount the next pocket 8¼ inches down, using the 5-inch by 8-inch card as a guide. (This pocket holds the bottom of the picture card).
7. Using the name tags as spacing guides, arrange the remaining six pockets.
8. Put Scotch tape down each edge to help hold the pockets.

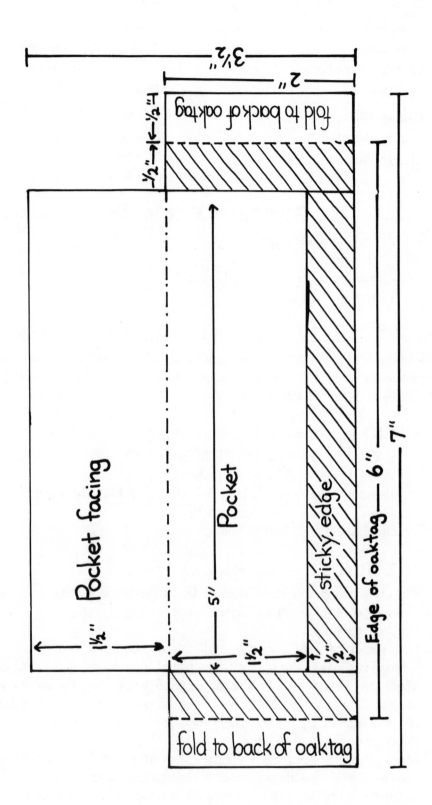

fold to back of oaktag

3½"

2"

½" ← ½"

½"

Pocket facing

Pocket

1½"

5"

sticky edge

1½"

½"

Edge of oaktag — 6"

7"

fold to back of oaktag

Durability

1. If it's worth making, it's usually worth making as durable as possible.

2. Laminating is a process that uses heat to adhere a thin plastic coating to both sides of a flat surface.

   a. A roller laminator applies plastic to both sides at once.

   b. Laminating can also be done with a dry mount press.

   c. Tips on laminating:

      1) Before laminating, use dry mount press or iron to thoroughly dry poster board or construction paper; otherwise it may bleed or have moisture pockets.

      2) Don't trim edges too closely — it may peel.

3. Contact paper is an adhesive-backed plastic. It has a paper backing which can be easily peeled off after the Contact is cut to a working size. It comes in a variety of colors. (Most of the uses of Contact in this book refer to the *clear*, not frosted, embossed, or colored, paper). Contact paper may be affected by heat and humidity. Put contact paper in the freezer for a few minutes before using; it peels more easily.

   a. Place Contact paper on flat surface, sticky side up. Lower one edge of the item to be covered to the Contact and slowly press the item to the Contact.

   b. If bubbles occur, they can usually be worked out to the edge by applying pressure with the rounded portion of a spoon, a cold iron, or finger tips. A pin prick may allow air to escape.

   c. When trimming, don't cut too close to the board. Rounding off corners helps games wear longer.

   d. It's best to cover both sides, but if only one side is to be covered, be sure to lap to the back side to prevent peeling.

   e. Cards for games can be covered as a unit, then cut apart.

Caution: Plastic covered games may be damaged by extended exposure to heat as in closed cars or on window sills.

Familiar Formats

Use the same familiar formats over and over. This means that once the child understands the rules for each format, he can concentrate on playing the game rather than learning new rules. Many simple games can be adapted to fit almost any center. For example: *Polka Dot Bear Color Puzzles* can become *Color Ghosts, Color Clowns,* and so on.

Familiar formats include:

- dot-to-dot
- lacing
- puzzle match
- peek and poke
- path games
- overwriting
- pocket
- puzzles

Familiar games include:

- Bingo
- Candyland
- Concentration
- Go Fish
- Lotto
- Old Maid
- Dominoes
- Tic Tac Toe

Felt Boards

1. Felt boards are extremely versatile and relatively inexpensive:
   a. Story telling and retelling
   b. Displaying sequence
   c. Practicing following directions
   d. Developing mathematical concepts and vocabulary
   e. Vocabulary development
   f. Wide assortment of commercially available materials
   g. Felt board materials are easily constructed by both teacher and children.
2. Materials that can be used on the felt board:
   a. Felt
   b. Synthetic interfacing (Pellon, medium weight, white). Pellon is available at most fabric stores.
      1) It is possible to trace an outline or pattern through Pellon.
      2) Pellon can be colored with colored pencils, crayon or markers.
      3) One piece of Pellon does not adhere to another for a layered picture (as Dress a Bear, Activity #2).
   c. Synthetic felt (Phun Phelt). This material is available in craft and fabric store, and it comes in many colors.
      1) It is easy to cut.
      2) One piece of synthetic felt does not adhere to another.
   d. Pictures
      1) Can be made by teacher or child or selected from catalogs, greeting cards, or magazines.
      2) can be backed with scraps of sandpaper, felt, or thin craft foam.

Felt Pens

1. Use water color markers under Contact paper. At times permanent markers bleed. The chemical make-up of ink and paper varies, so it is wise to test.
2. Use colors that show up well when writing words. Some colors (especially yellow) are hard to read.
3. Transparency pens work well for writing on Contact paper or laminated materials. They can be easily erased.
4. Permanent markers write on Contact paper or laminated materials. They do not rub off easily.
5. Game construction requires a variety of pens, both permanent and water-based, in many colors and point widths.
6. Crayons or colored pencils can be used under Contact paper and will not bleed or fade. They may also be laminated, but certain colors of crayons may run.

Game Boards

1. Make boards a fairly uniform size for easier storage. Few games need to be larger than 12 inches by 18 inches. File folders are ideal. Colored file folders make the game more attractive.
2. Make the board attractive, but don't overwhelm the child with wild colors or clutter. Add appropriate theme pictures. If the game is folded for storage, a picture on the front will attract the child.
3. Develop game boards with an open path to use with more than one set of cards such as letter recognition, color cards, sight words, numerals, shapes, and so on.
4. Plan ahead. Assemble needed materials. Block out a rough, full-sized version of the game. Keep this rough draft on file in case the game needs to be replaced or revised at a later date. See tissue paper tracing suggestions in Illustrations and Labels, Chapter 2.
5. Paths can be colored tape, small labels, rubber stamped, dots, or stickers. Consider using a small template for a pebble path, a shape path, or footprints. (A template may be cut from a margarine lid, using tape tabs for handles).
6. Good paths for young children are:
   a. modified Z, left to right, top to bottom progression, (see the illustration for *Honey Hunt*).
   b. clockwise movement around the outside edge (see the illustrations for *Teddy Bear March* and *Walk in the Forest*).

31

7. Avoid spiral paths which may confuse young children about the direction of the game.
8. Large game boards can be easily folded for storage if they are first cut in half, then taped.

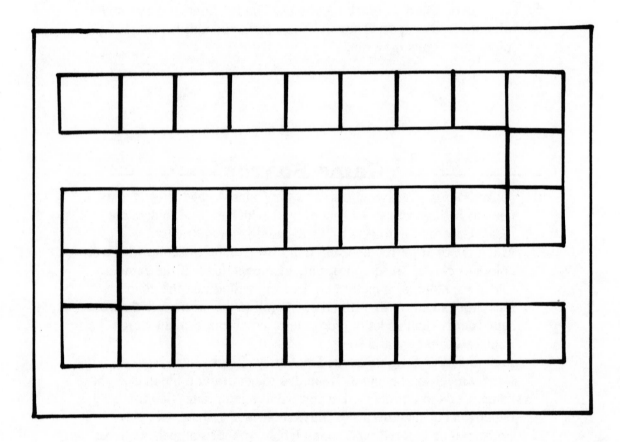

AVAILABLE PICTURES

- cartoon characters
- catalogs
- coloring books
- ditto sheets
- gift wrap
- greeting cards
- magazines
- picture stickers
- workbooks
- worn out books

ATTACHING PICTURES

1. Use rubber cement or spray adhesives to mount pictures smoothly.
2. Dry mount tissue works especially well for large pictures and for pictures to be puzzled.

TRACING FOR TRANSFER

If you want to copy a picture to put on a game:
1. Place white tissue paper over picture.
2. Trace picture with pencil.
3. Place tissue on gameboard and trace over pencil line with permanent marker(such as Sharpie).
4. Ink will go through tissue and make a faint outline on the board, which can then be re-traced.

ENLARGING AND REDUCING PICTURES

1. If you aren't violating copyright laws, copy machines easily and quickly enlarge and/or reduce pictures. Considering the value of personal time, the process is very inexpensive.
2. Opaque projectors work well when a very large picture is needed. (See *Bear Words* poster).
3. Graph paper can be used to enlarge or reduce some types of illustrations. One-inch graph paper works well for planning path games.

RUBBER STAMPS

A wide assortment of rubber stamps is available. Some that work well in game making are different sizes and styles of:

- alphabets
- shapes
- picture sets
- action sets
- novelty stamps
- foot print
- Teddy Bears

4. Using a brad, spinners can be attached:
   - to the traditional square,
   - directly to the game board
   - to a margarine tub lid(and keep game pieces inside).
5. A washer placed between the board surface and the brad sometimes makes the spinning easier.

DICE
1. Sponge cubes make interesting dice. Write on them with permanent markers.
2. Unfinished one-inch wooden cubes or blocks are easy to write on. Can be covered with clear nail polish.
3. For larger dice, cut two equal milk cartons as tall as they are square. Push the two together to form a cube. Cover with solid color contact. Colored tape or contact make good figures on the sides or write with permanent marker. (See *Movement Cubes*).

GAME CARDS
1. Small commercially available practice cards (2-inch by 3-inch) make good game cards.
2. End cuts from local printers of tag weight or cut index cards work well.
3. Cut off the upper left corner to help in sorting, in distinguishing the top from the bottom, and to keep the stack straight.
4. Consider using old playing cards.
5. Blank business cards.

PLAYING PIECES
1. Spools
2. Chips
3. Pennies
4. Teddy Bear Counters
5. Clothespins
6. Small novelty figures

————— Paper Cutting Tools —————

We have found the following tools helpful in preparation of games and activities in this book:

1. Paper drill. (One brand is Smead's, *Kwik Twist Paper Drill.*) They are available at office supply stores. This hand-operated tool punches a single hole in paper or cardboard wherever you want it.

34

2. Utility snips. They are available at office supply stores. Similar in shape to regular scissors, they are good for heavy cutting, including straight cuts on cardboard.
3. Exacto knife
4. Paper cutter
5. Standard single paper punch
6. Sharp standard scissors

Paper Products

boxes: flat, sturdy
- lids make good game boards.
- firm cardboard (14 ply)
- good for straight cut items

9-inch by 12-inch envelopes
- can be used as game boards
- pieces can be stored inside

file folders
- legal or letter size
- manila or colored

index cards
- lined and unlined
- in many colors

library pockets
- about 3 inches by 3 inches

mat board
- cannot be laminated; tends to split between layers
- good game board if contact is used

oak tag
- comes in manila and colors
- same weight as index cards

poster board
- colored on one side, gray on the back

practice cards (2 inches by 3 inches)
- available commercially
- could use blank business cards

railroad board
- heavier than posterboard
- colored on both sides

roll paper
- mural paper or butcher paper

sentence strip (3 inches by 24 inches)
- manila or colored

tag (oak tag)

LABELS AND STICKER DOTS

1. Labels and sticker dots make game making easier because:
   - they are available in many sizes, shapes and colors
   - they are relatively inexpensive
   - they can be written or drawn on and then applied to game
   - they make a good path
   - they can cover mistakes
   - they can be used in making games self-correcting
   - directions can be typed on a 3-inch by 5-inch label and affixed to the back of game
   2. If labels need to be applied after a game has been laminated or covered with Contact paper, use only press-apply labels.

——————— Lettering ———————

Helpful hints in lettering:
- Keep lettering simple, uncluttered.
- Follow your school's recommended style.
- Use lowercase letters whenever possible. (Close to 92 percent of what children are asked to read is lowercase).
- Select clear, easily visible colors.
- Provide a good model for beginning writers.

Avoid some pitfalls:
- Draw lines before you print.
- Plan and practice spacing with a pencil.
- Type or print on labels.
- Test out pens before writing on the game.
- Cut words from workbooks.
- Consider commercial rub-ons or stick-on letters.
- Use primary typewriter.

——————— Move Indicators ———————
And Playing Pieces

SPINNERS

1. Spinners can be constructed using heavy plastic (as from a gallon jug).
2. A safety pin makes a good spinner substitute.
3. Loose spinners can be purchased inexpensively from school suppliers.

Self-Checking

Materials that are self-checking:
- help children work independently
- build self-confidence
- teach children how to learn from materials
- give immediate feedback to the child
- save the teacher time, since the child does the checking.

Some ways to make games and activities self-checking are:
- answer on the back of a card
- answer card on the back of the folder
- cards numbered in sequence
- dot-to-dot to form
- electric board
- on the back of pairs
    matching colored marks
    matching dots
    matching pictures (stamps or stickers)
- overwrite
- puzzles
- two-piece puzzle

Sticky Stuff

Contact cement:
- for sticking plastic to plastic
- for sticking anything to laminated materials

dry mount tissue

glue:
- fabric glue
- glue sticks
- white glue

rubber cement:
- for attaching paper to paper smoothly

spray adhesive:
- for a light coat on a large surface

Storage

1. A set of boxes with lids, covered with a plain color of Contact paper can be used in more than one center. Place a clear Contact pocket on the lid to hold the game identifying card. (See *Contact Pocket*). When games are not being used in a center, they can be moved from the colored boxes to a plastic bag.

2. Plastic containers with lids hold some games well. Small margarine tubs hold playing pieces. Dishpans hold sets of file folders.
3. Plastic bags with tops that fasten (one brand is Ziploc), attached to games with yarn, hold playing pieces and cards.
4. Drawer organizers hold many small game pieces conveniently displayed in a center.
5. Plan the game to store easily. First find the box and design the game to fit the box. Use the inside of the box lid for the game board.
6. Storage containers can be coded by number or color for center organization.
7. Games can be drawn on the outside of large envelopes and pieces stored within.

Task Card Development

WHY?

Task cards help children become more independent in classroom activities. They are one method of providing sequential directions and/ or reinforcement without direct teacher involvement. However, they do not work well for all activities.

CONSTRUCTION

1. Keep the card very simple, brief, and uncluttered.
2. Title. The title identifies the activity or product. The title should be alone on the top line of the card for easy reference for both child and teacher.
3. Materials. Identify the materials list by writing the word *Use*. Picture the materials in a row below the title. Pictures may be drawn or cut from magazines. Label the pictures. Draw a line across the card under the materials list.
4. Directions.
   a. Identify the directions list by writing the word *Do*.
   b. Number the directions down the left side of the card.
   c. Each direction should include a picture and one word. Pictures should show the stages of development of the activity.
   d. Picture the activity in no more than five steps. (If the activity requires more than five main steps, it is probably too complicated to picture on a task card for independent work in a center by the young child).
   e. An end product may be illustrated in its simplest form.
      1) The simple model allows the least able child to succeed.
      2) The simple model frees the more capable child to be more elaborate.

Peanut Butter Playdough

Use: bowl spoon measuring cup honey

peanut butter MILK powdered milk

Do: 1. Mix 1 cup peanut butter + ½ cup honey + 1½ cup powdered milk

2. roll→ 12 balls

3. Shape O→ / or 😊 or 🐻 or ?

4. Show

5. Eat

See also additional task cards for *Paper Bag Puppet*, *Circle Bear*, *Circle Bear Teddy*, *Three Bears' House*, and *Finger Print Bear*.

Chapter Three

LANGUAGE ARTS ACTIVITIES

Language Activities Overview

This chapter includes activities which develop these language arts skills:

comprehension	sight words
letter recognition	visual
listening	vocabulary
oral language	writing

Language games included in this chapter are:

Abc Sequence Bears	Furnish a House
Alphabet Clothesline	Hug a Bear
b-e-a-r	Letter Sweater
b Wheel	Mama Bear, Baby Bear
Bear Bag	Matching Bears
Bear Body Puzzle	Picnic
Bear on a Chair	Polka-Dot Bears
Bear Words	Shopping with Mama Bear
Bears In and Out	Story Box
Body Word Puzzle	Story Teller
Color Bear Puzzle	Teddy Bear March
Concept Puzzle	Tic Tac Toe
Consonant Cottage	Touch and Tell
Dress a Bear	Walk in the Woods
	Write a Bear (Word)

Because puppets are such a good support of the language program and they can be used in so many ways, sample puppets have been included:

Introduction	Dancing Finger Puppet
Bear Finger Puppet	Glove Finger Puppet
Bear Hand Puppet	Paper Bag Puppet
Bear Mask	Paper Bag Puppet Task Card
Bear Stick Puppet	Pom-Pom Bear Stick Puppet
Dancing Felt Puppet	Wooden Spoon Puppet

Books for browsing are an integral part of almost every center. When children are interested in books during group activities, they often choose books independently. Both group and independent activities are included:

1. Literature Overview

2. Ways With a Good Book
The Three Bears

3. Choice Books and Activities
Browne, *Bear Hunt*
Douglas, *Good As New*
Freeman, *Corduroy*
Freeman, *A Pocket for Corduroy*
Kantrowitz, *Willy Bear*
Murphy, *Peace at Least*
Ormondroyd, *Theodore*
Pinkwater, *Bear's Picture*
Rockwell, *Albert B. Cub and Zebra*
Waber, *Ira Sleeps Over*
Wildsmith, *The Lazy Bear*

4. Flannel Board Story
The First Teddy Bear

5. Selected Bibliography

a-b-c Sequence Bears

Child places pieces in alphabetical order and assembles puzzle.

MATERIALS

- poster board or heavy tag (approx. 3 inches by 28 inches)
- markers
- tape
- scissors
- laminator or Contact paper

CONSTRUCTION

Tape three (or more) poster board strips together, overlapping ends at least 1½ inches. Trace and color 26 assorted bears on the long strip. Vary the color and pattern so that no two bears look exactly alike.

From left to right, label the bears alphabetically, a to z (lowercase). Laminate or cover with adhesive-backed paper.

Puzzle the strips uniquely between bears.

Alphabet Clothesline

Child hangs clothes on line in alphabetical order.

MATERIALS
- felt or pellon
- black permanent marker
- clothing patterns (see Dress a Bear, Chapter 3)
- tracing letters as desired
- snap clothespins
- clothesline (Venetian blind cord)

CONSTRUCTION
Using bear clothes patterns, trace and cut out 26 articles of clothing. With marker put one lowercase letter (a– z) on each article of clothing. To help the beginner, letters can also be written on clothespins.

PLAY
Using snap clothespins, child hangs lettered clothing on clothesline in alphabetical order. Variation: Child hangs up clothing with specific letter as directed by teacher.

Child matches letters to outlines.

MATERIALS

- file folder
- construction paper in six colors
- six markers to match the construction paper colors
- scissors
- pencils
- letter stencils, lowercase, in assorted styles and sizes
- laminator or Contact paper

CONSTRUCTION

Choose six styles of letter patterns. In pencil, trace b-e-a-r in each style on the file folder. (See illustration). Place each set of letters on a different color of construction paper. Trace, laminate, and cut out. Using a marker that corresponds in color to the construction paper letters, trace over the letter outlines on the file folder.

Child identifies words beginning like bear.

MATERIALS

- pizza cardboard wheel or poster board circle (8 inches)
- snap clothespins
- small pictures (most with "b" as initial sound)
- rubber cement
- laminator or Contact paper

CONSTRUCTION

Space pictures evenly around circle edge. Place bear picture in the center. Glue all pictures. Write the correct word on the back of the circle to identify each b picture. Laminate or cover with Contact.

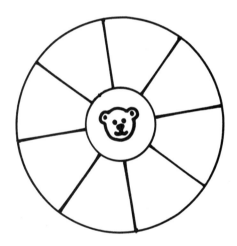

PLAY

Child snaps clothespin on each "b" picture and self-checks by looking at the back of the circle.

Variation: Words corresponding to the b pictures can be written on the clothespins. Child matches word to picture.

47

Bear Bag

Child names object from bag.

MATERIALS

- brown grocery bag or shopping bag with bear picture on it or box covered with bear gift wrapping.
- common objects:

brush	buttons	belt
bell	banana	bow
beads	bread	beads
ball	bear	box
	bulb	balloon

PLAY

Objects are placed in bag. Child removes an object from bag, names it, then tells a friend about it.

Variations:

1. Child classifies according to his own criteria.
2. Children are seated in a circle. Five to eight objects are removed from the bag and placed in the center of the circle. Children look at the objects for a few seconds, then shut their eyes. Leader goes around circle tapping children on the head. If tapped, the child goes to the center, takes one object, returns to his place and hides the object behind him. When all objects have been taken, the leader tells the children to open their eyes and chooses one child to be IT. IT tries to remember the objects and calls them back saying: "Come back, ball." "Come back, bell." If child cannot remember all items, other group members may help.

Bear Body Puzzle

Child assembles body parts to form Teddy Bear.

MATERIALS

- plastic placemat, brown on one side
- black permanent marker
- scissors

CONSTRUCTION

Trace and cut patterns from placemat. Label each body part, for example, "leg," "arm," and so on.

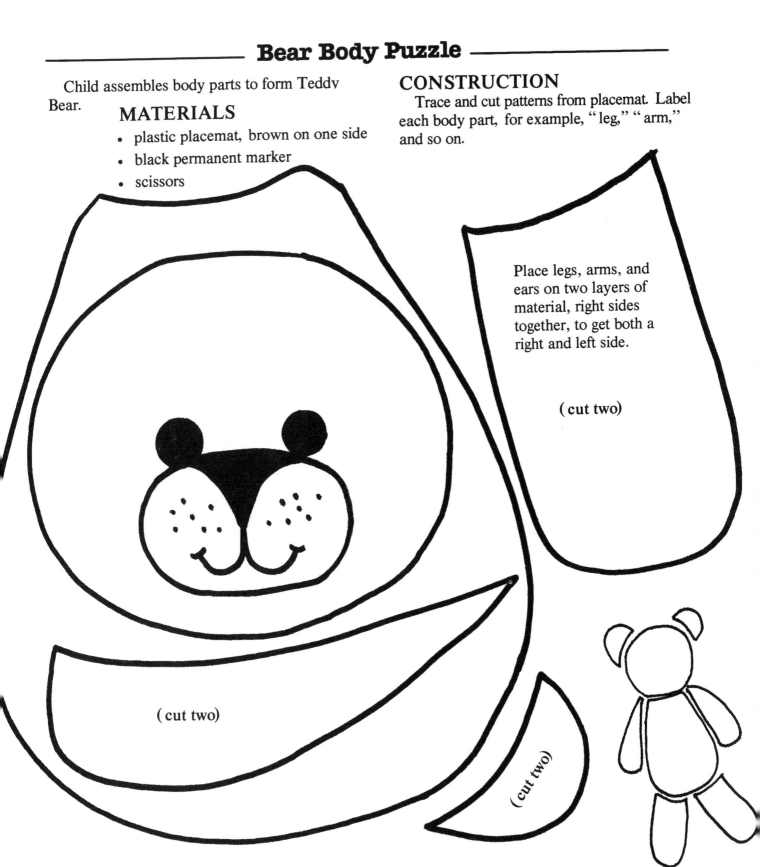

Place legs, arms, and ears on two layers of material, right sides together, to get both a right and left side.

(cut two)

(cut two)

(cut two)

49

Bear on a Chair

Child listens and follows directions.

MATERIALS

- Teddy Bear
- box
- chair

PROCEDURE

Children sit in a small group surrounding the Teddy Bear, the chair, and the box. One child gives a simple direction such as:

- Sit on the chair and hold the bear.
- Put the bear in the box and hop back to your place.
- Put the bear under the box and skip around it.

Suggestions:

- When a child has completed the directions correctly, ask those watching if he was right.
- Directions may be added as the children become more sophisticated.
- Add a toy.

Bear Words

Child participates in discussion of words describing Teddy Bears.

MATERIALS

- several Teddy Bears and Teddy Bear pictures
- chart paper (bear shaped or draw a large bear)
- marker

PROCEDURE

Discuss Teddy Bears. Teacher records words on chart. Consider putting head words on the head, paw words on the paw.

back	bear	eye	front
cub	furry	fuzzy	hug
fur	love	mouth	heart
leg	paw	round	soft
nose	tail	Teddy	
stomach	black	brown	

Variations:

- Chart may be displayed in the Teddy Bear center and children may dictate additional words as appropriate.
- Child may copy words from the chart.

50

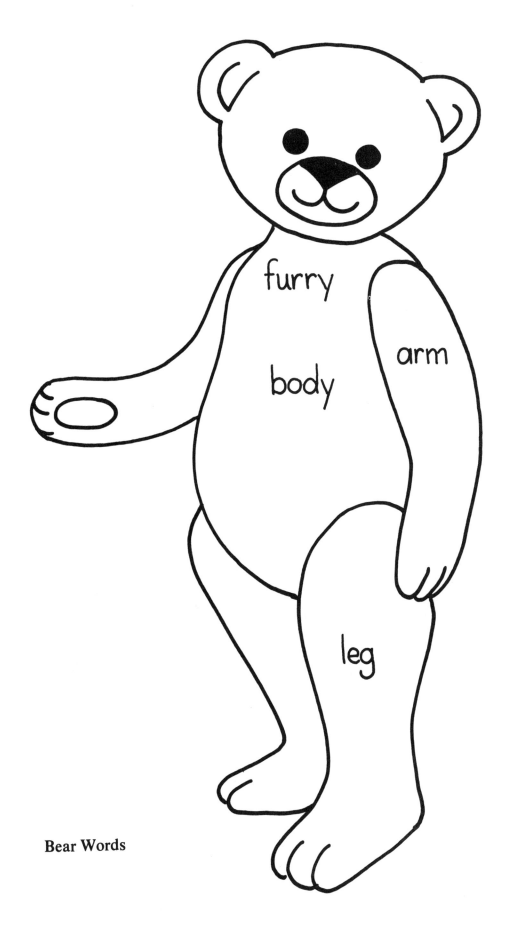

furry

arm

body

leg

Bear Words

51

Bears In and Out

Child plays cooperative game and practices "in" and "out."

MATERIALS

- 12 Teddy Bear Counters (Milton Bradley)
- blank 4-inch square commercial spinner (or make a spinner)
- black permanent marker
- small box
- solid color Contact paper
- scissors

CONSTRUCTION

Design spinner and box top as shown. Cover small box with Contact. Optional spinner construction: Cut spinner from margarine lid. Attach to box top using paper fastener. (Washers will help the spin).

PLAY (for two)

Each child takes four bears from the box, leaving the four remaining bears in the box. Children spin in turn, putting a bear in the box or taking one out as indicated by the spinner. (If the spinner shows "out of the box" and the box is empty at that time, the player misses that turn). Play continues until one player gets all of his bears in the box.

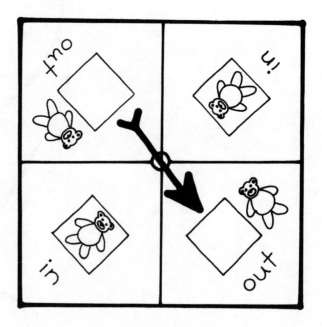

Bears In and Out

Body Word Puzzle

Child matches words with appropriate body parts in puzzle.

MATERIALS

- poster board (8½ by 11 inches)
- markers
- ruler
- scissors
- rubber cement (optional)
- Laminator or Contact paper

CONSTRUCTION

Reproduce the bear and words as shown in illustration. Trace on poster board or mount on poster board with rubber cement. Laminate or cover with Contact paper. Make a cut about 3 inches long on each dotted line. Puzzle vertically to make the word cards. The vertical cut should be irregular in order to provide a unique puzzle line for each word card.

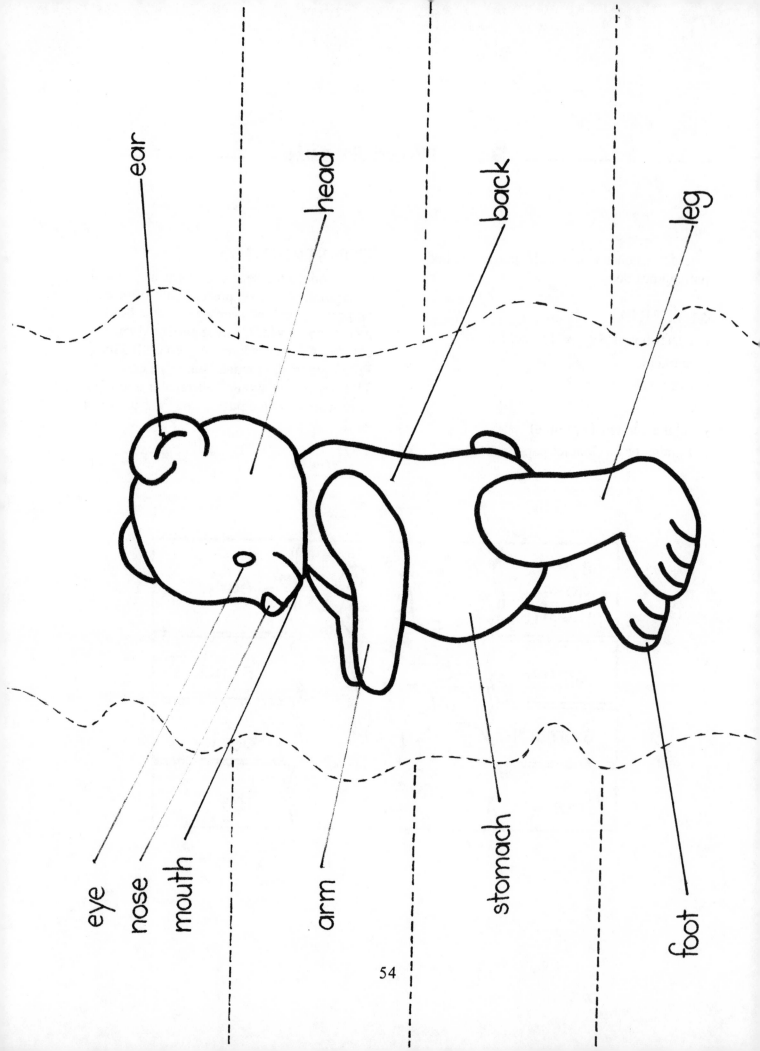

ear

head

back

leg

eye

nose

mouth

arm

stomach

foot

54

Color Bear Puzzles

Child matches colored bear to corresponding color word.

MATERIALS

- construction paper: red, orange, yellow, green, blue, purple, brown, black, pink white
- matching colored markers
- 5 - by-8 inch tag or poster board
- rubber cement
- scissors
- Laminator or Contact paper.

CONSTRUCTION

Cut one bear from each color of construction paper. Using rubber cement, glue one bear to the left side of each piece of poster board. On the right side of the card, print the color name in the corresponding color. Laminate or Contact. Puzzle each card uniquely into two pieces.

Child completes puzzle illustrating one concept.

MATERIALS

- large picture appropriate for puzzle or adapt Consonant Cottage (Chapter 3) or several bears or use sponge-backed plastic placemat with picture.
- mat board
- small press-apply labels
- fine line marker
- puzzle-sized box or file folder
- rubber cement or dry mount
- Exacto knife
- Contact paper

CONSTRUCTION

Decide on the appropriate size for the puzzle. This could be determined by the available box so the puzzle could be completed in the bottom; or use an available folder for a word background upon which the puzzle can be worked.

Color and trim the picture. Cut the mat board just larger than the picture so it will have a border. Mount picture on mat board with rubber cement or dry mount. Carefully plan puzzle cuts so the pieces will be interesting, but not confusing. Cut with Exacto knife.

Plan a variety of related words for the back of the puzzle, one for each pice. Depending upon your picture, you could write the name of the item pictured on each piece. (Write "window" on the back of the window).

As you plan your puzzle, make a word background upon which the puzzle can be worked. After you have cut apart your puzzle, draw around each piece so an outline of each piece appears on the background. If you use Consonant Cottage, consider these words: window, flowers, box, door, oval window, roof, chimney, bear. Write the words on labels for the back of the puzzle piece. Within each outline, write the same word that is on the back of the puzzle piece.

Variation: Use a larger plain color poster board or placemat. Plan carefully to cut in five pieces. A large numeral five (5) should be written on the centerpiece. On the front of each piece show the concept of five in a unique manner. Possible ways to show five are:

- five fingers (picture)
- five toes (picture)
- five pennies = one nickel (picture)
- five (the word *five*)
- 4 +1
- 3 +2
- 1 +1 +1 +1 +1
- 5:00 (as shown on clock face)
- five animals (picture)

Each child matches pictures with beginning consonants.

MATERIALS
- poster board for six houses (6 by 9 inches)
- six strips of cardboard (2 by 8 inches)
- tape
- oak tag or colored poster board for bears
- assorted markers
- tiny pictures (from old workbooks, stickers)
- laminator or Contact paper.

CONSTRUCTION
1. Cottages. Reproduce six cottages. Write one lowercase consonant (e.g., b, m, f, g, s, t) in the oval window. Decorate with markers. Laminate or Contact. Cut slit. Attach the easel near the roof peak with tape so the house can stand. (See drawing).
2. Bears. Make 18 bears from oak tag or colored poster board (three per cottage). Choose three tiny pictures for each letter on the house. Glue a picture on each bear so that three bears can "live" in each cottage. To make the game self-checking, write the beginning letter on the back of each bear. Make a face on each bear. Laminate or cover with Contact.

Consonant Cottage

glue
fold

back view

- - - - Cut out here - - - - - - -

Dress a Bear

Child dresses bear.

MATERIALS

- brown and tan felt for bear
- pellon and crayons or assorted colors of felt
- scissors
- glue
- permanent markers

CONSTRUCTION

1. Construct brown felt bear with tan muzzle and use marker for face details.
2. Make at least three sets of clothing in a variety of colors and/or designs. (Clothing may be labeled with color words or clothing words.)

PLAY

Child dresses bear independently.

Variation: Child follows directions of another. Directions can be more difficult if the clothing is quite similar such as: red shirt with blue stripe, blue shirt with red stripe.

Variation: Weather Bear. Make a variety of clothes appropriate for different weather.

Dress A Bear Alternate
Clothes Spin

Child spins to dress bear appropriately.

MATERIALS

- two sets of bears and clothing
- spinner, cube or dice (see Move Indicators, Chapter 2)

CONSTRUCTION

1. Cut out two (or more) bears and sets of clothing. Divide the spinner into five parts and draw a miniature bear or an article in each square.
2. Spinner. Use a blank commercial spinner or construct a spinner. Divide the spinner into five parts and draw a miniature bear or an article of clothing in each section. To make the game easier, one section on the spinner could be a "free" space.

PLAY

Bears and clothing are placed between two children. Each child spins in turn until he spins a bear. Child spins for clothing, one spin per turn.

Variation. Use a wooden cube and draw miniature clothing on each side.

Variation. Use a die and number the bear 1, the clothing 2, 3, 4, 5, and 6.

Dress a Bear

61

Furnish a House

PROCEDURE

1. Child looks through several versions of *Goldilocks and The Three Bears,* paying close attention to the furnishings of the bears' house.
2. Child divides paper into four parts by drawing vertical and horizontal lines or folding paper.
3. Child looks through available magazines and catalogs and chooses appropriate lines or folding paper.
4. Child cuts out pictures and glues them in the " house."
5. Child compares his or her furnishings to that in the stories.

Child selects appropriate house furniture.

MATERIALS

- manila paper (12 inches by 18 inches)
- crayons
- scissors
- glue
- magazines and / or catalogs
- several versions of *Goldilocks and The Three Bears.*

Hug A Bear

RATIONALE: For some children, this can be one of the most successful activities of the center. It is completely undemanding and non- competitive. It gives the child who needs or wants this type of contact the opportunity to just relax and be him/herself. It gives a child a way to complete one bear activity successfully. When a child first visits a center, it may hold his or her attention long enough for him or her to get interested in other center activities.

Child hugs a bear.

MATERIALS

- Teddy bears
- rocking chair (optional)

PLAY

This activity is just what the name implies: the opportunity for a child to simply hold and love a Teddy bear.

Letter Sweater

Child traces letter on bear's sweater.

MATERIALS

- oak tag or poster board
- markers
- scissors
- laminator or Contact paper

CONSTRUCTION

Trace or copy bears on tag. Make one for each letter to be practiced. Color bears if desired. Print a different letter on each bear, using yellow or orange marker. Laminate or cover with Contact paper. Cut out.

Construction Variation: Instead of cutting out the bears, draw lines on the left side of the bear master so they correspond to your writing paper and duplicate the page. Print a different letter on each bear, using yellow or orange marker. Laminate or cover with Contact. Child traces the letter on the sweater and uses the lines to practice.

Variation: Write numerals, draw basic shapes or simple designs.

Letter Sweater

Mama Bear, Baby Bear

Child matches capital letter to lower case letter.

MATERIALS

- poster board: several shades of bear colors, including brown, beige, yellow, ginger, and white
- black marker
- labels (about 1 inch by 1½ inch)
- scissors
- lettering size guide or stick-on letters
- laminator or Contact paper

CONSTRUCTION

Cut out 26 mama and 26 baby bears. (Mama and baby should be the same color). Draw in faces. Put the 26 capital letters on the front of the large bears and on the BACK of the small bears. Put the 26 lowercase letters on the front of the baby and on the BACK of the mama. (Be sure to use a lettering size guide or stick-on letters or write on a label). Laminate or cover with Contact paper.

Mama Bear, Baby Bear— Alternate Construction

MATERIALS

- four colors construction paper: brown, beige, yellow, ginger
- 26 poster board cards (5 inches by 8 inches)
- marker
- lettering guide
- laminator or Contact paper

CONSTRUCTION

Make two-piece puzzles. Choose a mama bear and baby bear pattern that will fit on a 5-inch-by-8-inch poster board. Use rubber cement to glue the construction paper bears to the poster board. Letter matching bears "C c." Laminate or cover with Contact paper. Puzzle each card uniquely.

Mama Bear, Baby Bear

Matching Bears

Child matches the bear to the outline or color bear to a color word.

MATERIALS

- oak tag
- file folder: manila, gray or white
- colored markers: eight basic colors
- circle stickers: eight white self-adhesive (¾ inch)
- eight unique bear patterns
- black fine line marker
- laminator or Contact paper

CONSTRUCTION

1. Reproduce the eight bears on oak tag. Use markers to color one bear each of the basic colors. Laminate or cover with Contact paper. Cut out.
2. Use bears as tracing patterns and draw outline of each bear on the file folder. Label each outlined bear with the appropriate color word.
3. Color the circle stickers with the eight basic colors. Place them in a vertical line down the left side of the folder. Print the color word beside the circle. Laminate or cover folder with Contact paper.

PLAY

Using either the color words or the outlines as clues, the child matches the bears to the appropriate outline.

Matching Bears

Picnic

Child assembles a meal for three bears.

MATERIALS
- assorted construction paper
- three file folders
- oak tag
- markers
- scissors
- Contact paper or laminator

PLAY EQUIPMENT
- three large paper plates
- three pie-sized paper plates
- three paper cups
- three settings of plastic silverware
- three napkins

CONSTRUCTION
1. Bowls. From assorted construction paper, cut one of each size. Label: "Papa," "Mama," and "Baby." With marker, complete bowl details so food will fit on bowl. Laminate or Contact.
2. Placemats. Draw around dishes on the placemat. Label. Laminate or Contact.
3. Food
   a. Porridge: From oak tag, cut one mound of each size. Label on front or back.
   b. Blueberries: From blue construction paper, cut one mound each size. Label on front or back. For added interest, draw berry-sized circles with a dark marker.
   c. Fish: From tan construction paper, cut one of each size.
   d. Biscuits: From oak tag, cut three circles: small, medium and large.
   e. Honey: From yellow construction paper, cut three irregular blobs: small, medium and large.
   f. Food should be laminated or covered with Contact paper. Store food pieces in separate envelopes. Label envelope, e.g., "Berries."

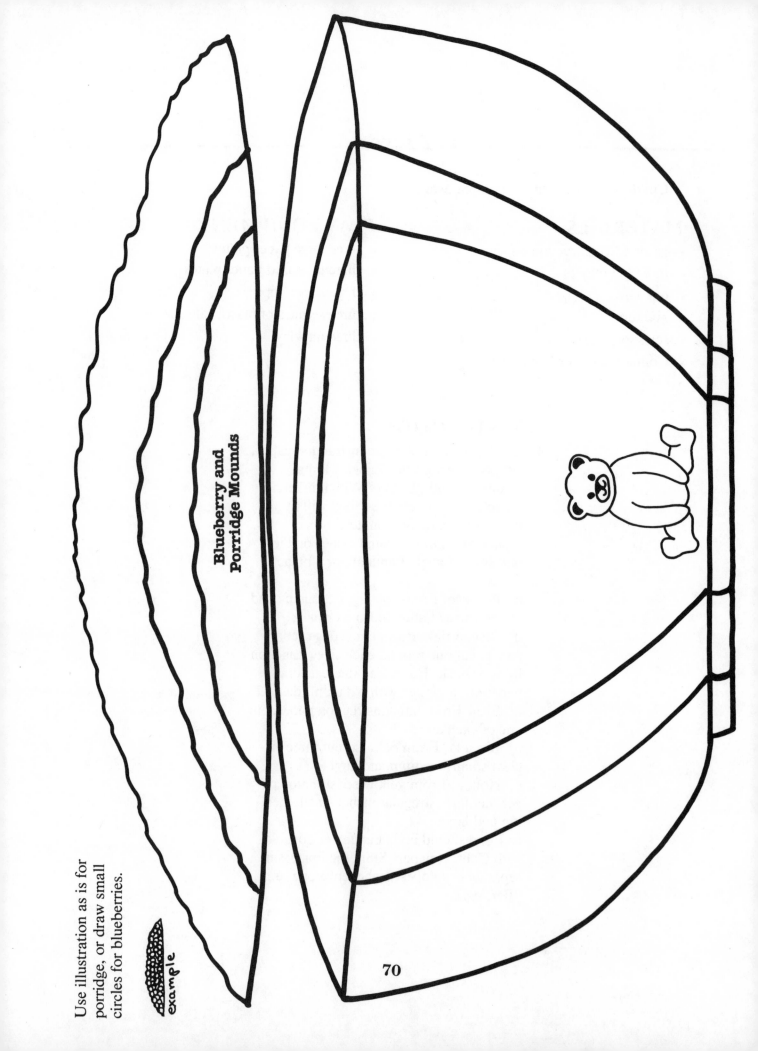

Use illustration as is for porridge, or draw small circles for blueberries.

example

Blueberry and
Porridge Mounds

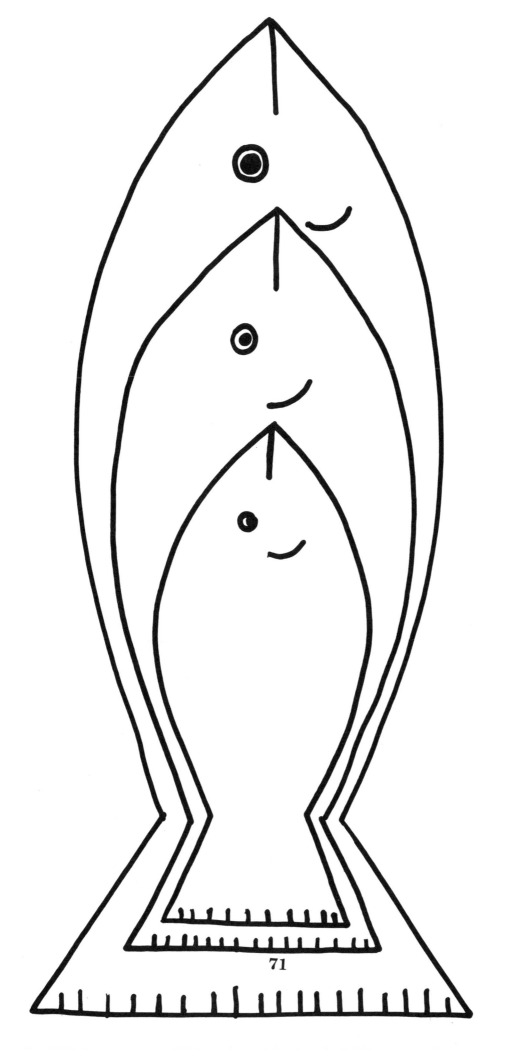

71

Blueberries

Biscuits

honey

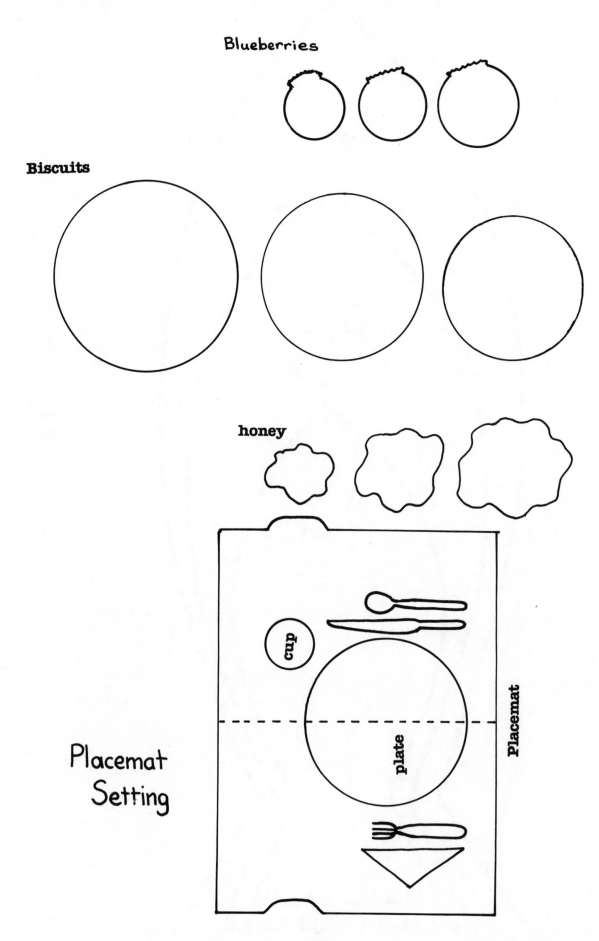

Placemat
Setting

cup

plate

Placemat

72

Polka-Dot Bears

Child sorts puzzle pieces by color and puts puzzles together.

MATERIALS

- construction paper (red, orange, yellow, green, blue, purple, brown, black, pink, white) (can be mounted on tag or poster board)
- white circle stickers (¾ inch)
- markers
- scissors
- dry mount tissue or rubber cement
- laminator or Contact paper

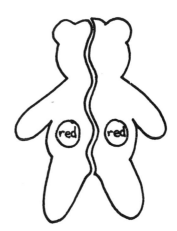

CONSTRUCTION

1. Cut one bear from each color of construction paper. Draw lines to puzzle each bear uniquely. Vary the number of pieces from two to ten. The easiest puzzles should be red, blue, and yellow.
2. Attach one sticker to each puzzle piece so that it will be easy to identify the front side of the bear. With marker that matches the bear color, print the color word on each sticker. Laminate or Contact.
3. Cut on lines to puzzle each bear.
4. On the outside of an envelope or box, put an outline of the bear for those needing a pattern to follow.

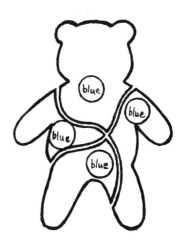

Shopping With Mama Bear

Child listens and responds to directions given by another child.

MATERIALS
- basket with handle
- assortment of real, empty grocery containers or play groceries or pictures of groceries

PLAY
Child pretends to be Mama or Papa Bear on a trip to the grocery store. Another child gives a verbal list of items to be put in basket.
Variations:
1. Very short list (two or three items)
2. Longer list (four to eight items)
3. Several items for a picnic
4. Several items all one color
5. Several items in one food group
6. One item from each food group
7. Items for one meal

Story Box

Child will use box items during dramatic play.

MATERIALS
- clothing for three bears and Goldilocks
- hats
- wigs
- bowls, spoons
- small sheets or blankets for bedding

PLAY
Children choose items from the box for spontaneous production of *Goldilocks and the Three Bears.*

Variation. Additional objects are placed in the box to help children act out other stories or pretend situations.

Child retells a story.

MATERIALS

- Selection of well-known and /or appealing new books such as:
  Douglas, *Good As New*
  Flack, *Ask Mr. Bear*
  Freeman, *Corduroy*
  Goldilocks and the Three Bears (several versions)
  Martin, *Brown Bear*
  McCloskey, *Blueberries for Sal*
  Morris, *Goodnight Dear Monster*
  Murphy, *Peace at Last*
  Ormondroyd, *Theodore*
  Waber, *Ira Sleeps Over*
- Specific materials for activities as listed below.

PROCEDURE

Place materials in the center which encourage the child to retell stories previously heard during class storytime, on records / tapes at a listening station, or during filmstrips or movies.

1. Child may simply retell the story to another child using his own words. He may or may not use a book to provide picture clues.
2. Felt board. Pictures can be backed with sandpaper or felt scraps so they will adhere to the felt board. Child uses available materials to retell the story:
   - commercial flannel board sets such as *Goldilocks and the Three Bears*
   - felt or Pellon figures (teacher-made)
   - figures cut from catalogs or magazines
   - child /teacher drawn pictures
3. Child retells story using pictures cut from worn-out or inexpensive books mounted and laminated on tag or posterboard. Pictures may be numbered on back so that the child can check sequential order. Sequence can also be checked by having an identical whole book available.
4. Dramatization. Costumes and some props in the center will help initiate spontaneous performances by one child or a small group. These performances could be repeated for the total class if the cast is willing.
5. Puppets. The presence of appropriate puppets will stimulate story retelling. Use commercial, teacher-made or child-made puppets. See puppet section for ideas for simple puppet construction ideas.
6. Illustration. Art supplies within the center allow the interested child the opportunity to illustrate a favorite story in a variety of ways.

Variations. After the child's independent retelling experiences, the teacher could encourage the child to experiment with the story by:

- changing the original by using different characters
- interchanging characters from two different stories
- trying different settings
- changing the personality of a character
- changing the ending of the story

Child identifies colors.

MATERIALS

- two Teddy Bear Counters (Milton Bradley)
- file folder (legal or lettersize, color of choice)
- markers
- ruler
- pencil
- spinner
- press apply labels (½ inch by ¾ inch) if desired
- laminator or Contact paper

CONSTRUCTION

1. Gameboard. Reproduce accompanying path pattern on file folder. (See Game Board suggestions and Illustration suggestions, Chapter 2). Put a bear picture in the center area of the game as shown. Put a similar picture on the front of the folder. Print the game title on the board, on the front of the folder and on the tab. Use markers to color in the squares. Choose colors according to the practice needs of the students. Laminate or cover folder with Contact paper.

2. Spinner. Use a commercial spinner or one made on the lid of a margarine tub. Divide the spinner into six sections with black lines. Write a number (1, 2, or 3) in each section. Note: Spinner could be drawn directly on the game board with the spinner arrow (available commercially) attached with a paper fastener.

PLAY

Each child, in turn, spins, then moves his marker bear that number of spaces and identifies the color of the space. If he is unable to identify the color, he goes back one space. The winner is the child who reaches the end of the game path first.

Variation. Game may be constructed for three levels of difficulty by:
a) coloring path squares (as directed above)
b) printing upper or lower case letters on labels mounted in upper left corner of each colored square
c) printing sight words on labels mounted in lower right corner of each colored square

The child can then spin, move, and according to his level of play, identify the color, the letter, or the sight word.

76

start →

finish

Teddy Bear March

Tic Tac Toe

Child identifies letters while playing a traditional game.

MATERIALS

- 12-inch-by-12-inch railroad board or cardboard (yellow, white or orange)
- oak tag for ten bears
- bear pattern (about 3 inches) (See small Stick Puppet pattern, Puppet Pages)
- markers: brown, orange, black
- ruler
- scissors
- razor blades
- ten ½-inch round metal washers
- nine 1-inch strip magnets
- Contact cement
- laminator or Contact paper
- Practice cards (2 inches by 3 inches) (or cut index cards)
- nine library pockets (3 inches by 3 inches)

CONSTRUCTION

1. Board. Use a ruler and a black marker to divide the board into nine Tic Tac Toe squares, each 4 inches by 4 inches. Laminate or Contact.
2. Pockets. Laminate or Contact. Slit openings with a razor blade. Use Contact cement to attach one pocket in each square on the board. Use Contact cement to attach 1-inch magnet strips to pockets.
3. Bears. Reproduce ten bears on oak tag. Color five brown, five orange. Add facial features with the black marker. Laminate or Contact. Use Contact cement to attach one metal washer to the back of each bear.
4. Cards. Use the black marker to write the lower case letters, a to z, on 26 cards (2 inches by 3 inches). On another set of cards, write the upper case alphabet. Draw an orange line across the top of each lower case alphabet card, a brown line across the top of each upper case card. (This enables the children to sort cards easily as well as preventing top-bottom confusion.) Laminate or Contact all cards.

PLAY

Place nine letter cards in the pockets. Two children play, each choosing a bear color. In turn, each child pulls a card from a pocket. If he is able to identify it, he places one of his bears on the pocket. If not, the card is replaced in the pocket. The other child takes a turn. The object of the game is as in Tic Tac Toe, to place three bears in a row vertically, horizontally, or diagonally.

Variation. Cards may be numerals, 1–20, shapes, colors/color words, or beginning sight vocabulary. Play procedure remains the same.

Tic Tac Toe

Touch and Tell

Child describes the bear to another child.

MATERIALS
- variety of Teddy Bears
- blindfold

PROCEDURE
Child is blindfolded and handed a bear. The child describes as many characteristics of the bear as possible, using only "touch" clues.

Walk in the Woods

Child identifies beginning sight words.

MATERIALS
- posterboard (18 inches by 28 inches)
- Teddy Bear Counters, three of different colors (Milton Bradley)
- white tissue paper
- pencil
- markers
- bear stickers (if desired)
- practice cards (2 inches by 3 inches)
- ruler
- four circle templates (8-inch, 10-inch, 12-inch, 14-inch)
- laminator or Contact paper

CONSTRUCTION
Game Board
1. See GAME BOARD suggestions, (Chapter 2)
2. Use the four circle templates to develop the game path on the posterboard
3. Add space lines with rulers
4. Use markers to "landscape" the board.
5. Print the title on the board
6. Laminate or cover with Contact paper
7. To fold, cut in half and tape with wide clear tape or a strip of Contact paper.

Cards
1. Print or type beginning sight words on the cards. Choose words according to the reading series being used.
2. Write the numerals 1, 2, or 3 in the lower right corner of the card to indicate the number of spaces to move.
3. Cut off the upper left corner of each card. Draw a green line across the top of each card to help children sort cards.
4. Laminate or cover with Contact paper.

PLAY
Three children play, each choosing a bear color. In turn, each child draws a card, reads the word on the card, and if correct, moves clockwise the number of spaces indicated on the card. If the child is unable to read the word, he stays on the same space. The winner is the child who moves around the complete path first.

Variations: Cards may be numeral recognition, 1 – 20 (or higher), lower or upper case alphabet, colors or shapes. The playing procedure remains the same.

A Walk in the Woods

Finish

Start →

80

Write a Bear (Word)

Child practices manuscript handwriting by copying bear words.

MATERIALS

- tag board or 5-inch-by-8-inch index card
- writing paper
- rubber cement or dry mount tissue
- marking pens (thin line) or transparency pens
- laminator or Contact paper

CONSTRUCTION

Use standard writing paper and glue to the tag (or card) or line as shown below. Laminate or cover with Contact paper. For writing on cards, children may use crayons, grease pencils, or water base markers.

Variations:
1. Write child's name.
2. Write child's phone number.

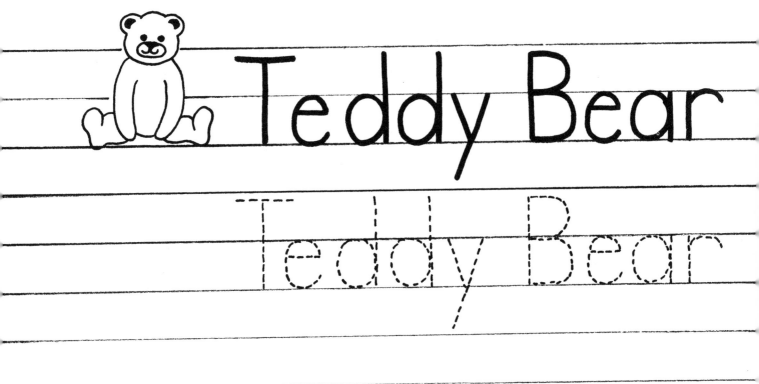

Puppet Pages

Puppets are a most valuable learning tool in the Early Childhood classroom. It is important that children have access to a variety of puppets, both commercial and teacher-made. It is also important that the children have the opportunity and materials available to create unique personal puppets.

Adults working with young children need to remember that the construction of a puppet is *not* the end goal of such a project. Emphasis should be on the performance of the puppet. Whether the puppet is used to retell a story, create a new story, express feelings, or reinforce a concept or skill being taught, the manipulation of the puppet and its personality development are the desired outcome of the construction. It is only when the child gives life to the puppet that the child's skills will be developed.

MATERIALS

- tag board or cardboard
- markers
- scissors
- glue or tape
- Contact paper or laminator

CONSTRUCTION

Select and cut out the bear finger puppet from oak tag. Color. Contact or laminate as desired. Curl the tabs around and glue or tape.

Bear Hand Puppet

MATERIALS

- felt: brown, black, tan
- black marker
- scissors
- fabric glue

CONSTRUCTION

Cut out pattern pieces. Glue the tan pieces in place. Glue the ears in place between the body pieces. Join the front and back by machine stitching, hand stitching, or gluing.

Nose
Cut one tan

Eyes
Cut two tiny black circles

Ears
Cut two brown

Cut two brown

Body

Inside ears

Cut two tan

Stomach
Cut one tan

Place dotted line on fabric fold when cutting out body.

Place on fold when cutting stomach.

84

Bear Hand Puppets

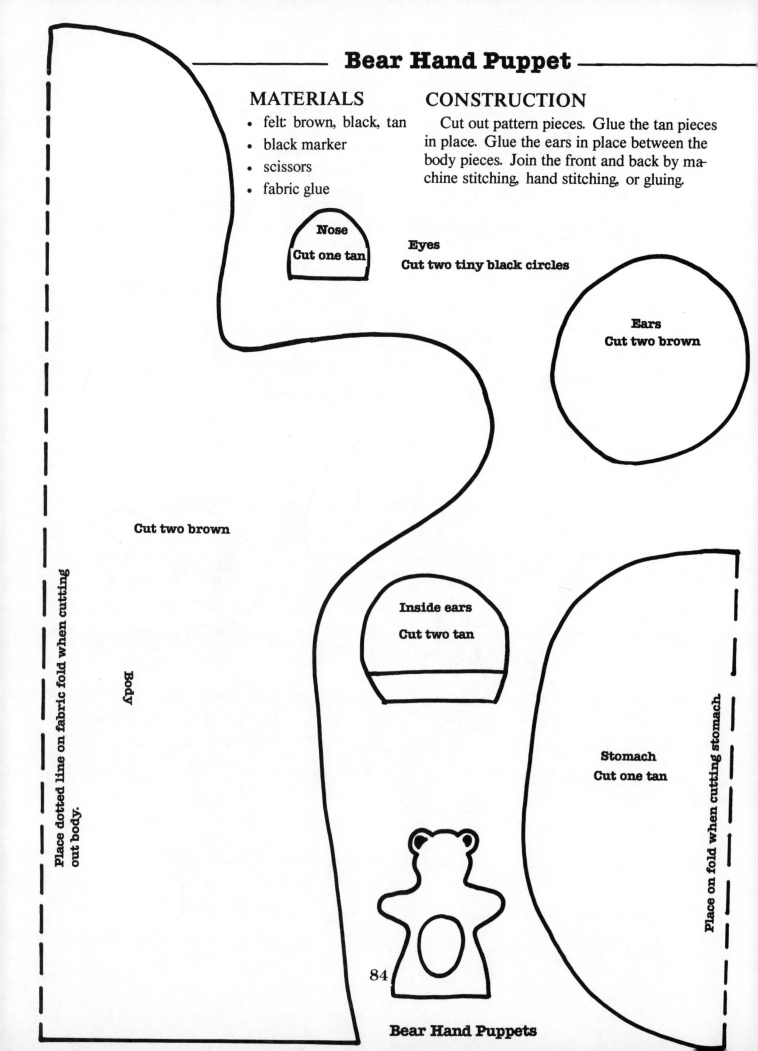

Bear Mask

MATERIALS
- brown poster board
- tan construction paper
- black markers
- scissors
- glue
- laminator or Contact paper

CONSTRUCTION

Trace the pattern pieces (extend neck for handle) and cut out. Outline pieces in black marker. Glue nose piece onto head. Draw eyes and nose on face. Cut out the eyes so the child can see. Cover with Contact or laminate.

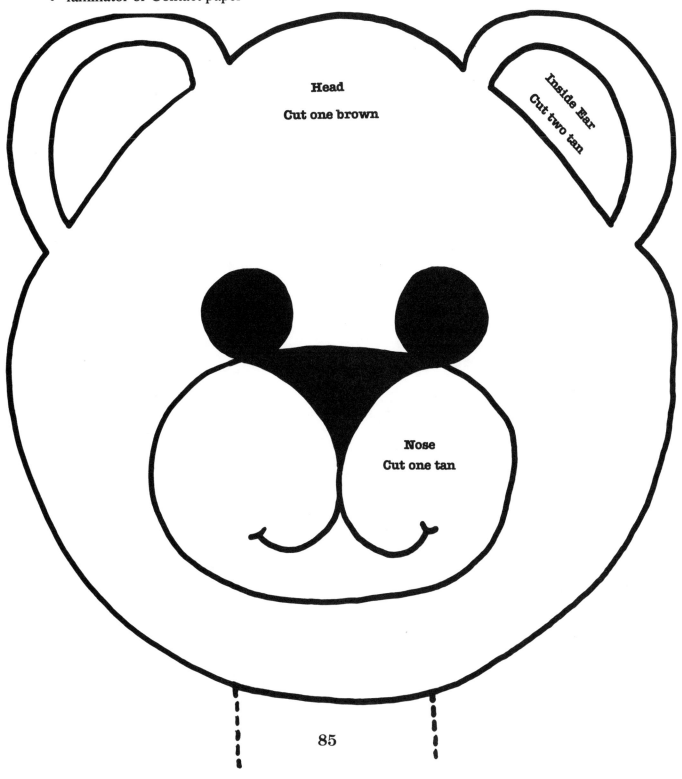

Head

Cut one brown

Inside Ear
Cut two tan

Nose
Cut one tan

85

Bear Mask

Bear Stick Puppets

MATERIALS

- bear pictures or old bear greeting cards
- tag board
- markers
- scissors
- glue
- sticks: tongue depressors or popsicle sticks
- Contact or laminator

CONSTRUCTION

Trace and cut any of the bear patterns or bears from catalogs, greeting cards or other picture sources. Mount them on tag board as appropriate. Color and glue on stick. Cover with Contact paper or laminate as desired.

Bear Stick Puppets

Bear Stick Puppets

Dancing Bear Felt Puppets

MATERIALS
- brown and tan felt
- two movable eyes
- pom-poms: medium brown, small black
- fiberfill stuffing
- pencil
- scissors
- fabric glue

CONSTRUCTION
1. Trace and cut all pattern pieces. Glue on the tan features. At the back waist, cut a slit allowing for seams. Join the outside edges all the way around by machine stitching, hand stitching or gluing.
2. Stuff the top of the body with fiberfill and glue at the waist so the top half will be closed. The slit will be open so the hand can be inserted in the *bottom* half with fingers in the feet to make him walk.
3. Glue on the movable eyes and the brown pom-pom. Glue the small black pom-pom on the brown pom-pom for the nose.

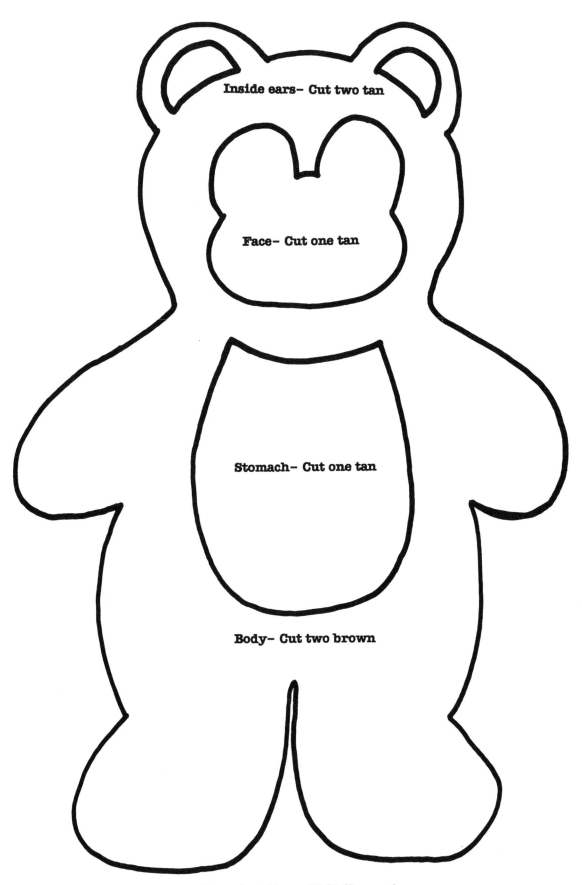

Inside ears– Cut two tan

Face– Cut one tan

Stomach– Cut one tan

Body– Cut two brown

Dancing Bear Felt Puppet

89

MATERIALS
- tag board or cardboard
- markers
- scissors
- glue
- Laminator or contact paper

CONSTRUCTION

Copy patterns onto tag board or cardboard. Cut one backing and one face for each puppet. Decorate bear faces. Cut out finger holes. Glue bear face onto backing. Laminate or cover with Contact paper as desired.

Backing for puppets.
(Cut one per puppet.)

cut out

cut out

MATERIALS

- finger from an old glove or surgitube (gauze finger bandage)
- felt scraps
- scissors
- glue
- marker

CONSTRUCTION

Make the bear's features out of felt. Glue on to the glove finger. Include ears, paws, and stomach as desired.

Variation: Use the entire glove. Put Goldilocks on index finger, Papa Bear on middle finger, Mama Bear on ring finger, and Baby Bear on the little finger.

Glove Finger Puppet

Paper Bag Puppet

Child creates a bear puppet.

MATERIALS
- 5-pound paper bag, white or brown
- bear pattern if desired
- crayons
- scissors
- glue
- task card

CONSTRUCTION
1. Color bear face and bag as desired.
2. Cut out upper and lower portions.
3. Glue lower portion of face on bag, straight edge against the fold under the bottom flap.
4. Make an oval of glue on the bottom of the bag. Attach the upper face so that the mouth sections are in alignment.

Paper Bag Puppet

Paper Bag Puppet

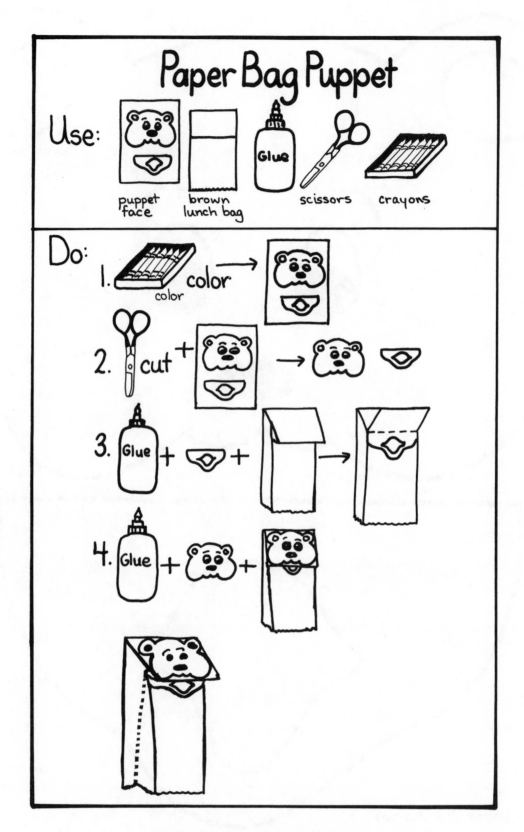

Use: puppet face | brown lunch bag | Glue | scissors | crayons

Do:
1. color color →
2. cut + →
3. Glue + + →
4. Glue + +

Paper Bag Puppet Task Card

Pom-Pom Bear Stick Puppets

MATERIALS

- tongue depressor (available drug store, craft stores)
- pom-poms: one large brown (head); one medium tan (nose and mouth); two small brown (ears); two small black (nose tip)
- two movable eyes
- glue

CONSTRUCTION

Glue the head onto the tongue depressor. Glue the nose just below the middle of the head. Glue the ears, nose tip, and movable eyes.

Pom-Pom Stick Puppet

Wooden Spoon Puppets: Goldilocks and the Three Bears

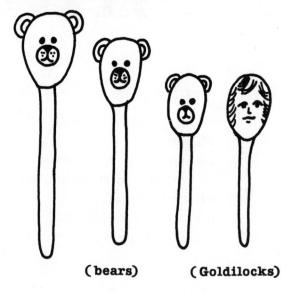

(bears)   (Goldilocks)

MATERIALS

- four wooden spoons, graduated sizes
- felt: brown, tan, pink
- yarn: yellow for hair, red for bow
- black marker
- scissors
- glue

CONSTRUCTION

1. Bears: Cut out all pattern pieces. Glue inside ear piece on to each ear Glue ears to convex side (outside) of spoons. Glue nose pieces to the middle of the bears' faces. With marker, add eyes, noses, mouths, and freckles onto faces. Glue faces to spoons.

2. Goldilocks: Cut out face. With marker, add eyes and mouth. Glue face on to convex side (outside) of spoon. To form hair, glue yellow yarn on both front and back of spoon. Glue little red bow in hair.

Face (Size of face will vary depending on spoon side)

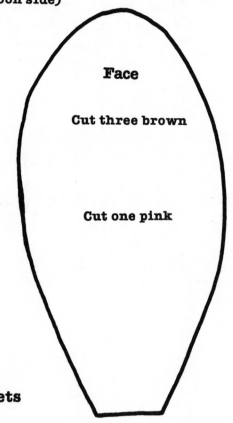

Face

Cut three brown

Cut one pink

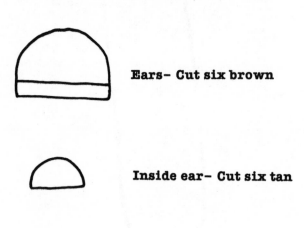

Ears- Cut six brown

Inside ear- Cut six tan

Nose- Cut three tan

Wooden Spoon Puppets

LITERATURE OVERVIEW

The importance of quality books in the life of the young child cannot be over-emphasized. Their value and contribution to the development of language abilities and attitudes toward the reading experience must be a primary concern in the planning of activities and programs.

A time for browsing in books, for information or pleasure reading, and for teacher storytime should be a *scheduled* part of each day's activities for the young child.

Emphasis should be placed on the meaning, interpretation and application of what is read. Solicit the active contributions of the child through discussions, creative dramatics, art, music or other forms of expression. All of these offer tremendous possibilities for language development.

Ways with a Good Book

There is no doubt that the story of *Goldilocks and the Three Bears* is one of the best-known of traditional stories. Every child is familiar with some version of this classic. Because of its popularity, *Goldilocks and the Three Bears* is an ideal work to help children enjoy and appreciate literature. This classic will be used to illustrate a variety of literature activities. All of the examples given would probably not be used with one book.

I. Introducing Books
    A. Acknowledge the title, the author, and the illustrator during the introduction.
    B. Books may be introduced by:
        1. showing story illustrations
        2. talking about the title or book
        3. having children discover a staged scene
            a. three bowls
            b. set table
        4. getting acquainted with one character
            a. role play Goldilocks
            b. talk using a bear puppet
        5. discovering the book on a ledge or story area
        6. commenting about the book (The teacher says, "When I was little . . .")
        7. comparing one to another orally
            a. compare versions of *Goldilocks and the Three Bears*.
            b. compare *Goldilocks and the Three Bears* to other bear books.

II. Retelling
    A. After hearing the story one or more times, a child will retell the story.
        1. First-time retelling should follow the original storyline with the same setting, plot development, and characters.
        2. Emphasis should be placed on correct sequence of events.
        3. Additional retelling could offer variations of the story.
    B. Child may utilize any of the following aids or techniques for retelling:
        1. Felt board.
            a. Use felt or Pellon figures, child-drawn pictures or figures cut from catalogues or magazines.
            b. Pictures can be backed with sandpaper or felt so they will adhere to the felt board.

2. Dramatization.
   a. Performances may be spontaneous or rehearsed with a small group of children.
   b. There may nor may not be a narrator.
   c. Costumes and props should be available.
   d. Performances could be videotaped.
3. Puppets.
   a. Use commercial, teacher-made, or child-made puppets.
   b. See *Puppet Pages* (Chapter 2) for simple puppet construction ideas.
4. Illustrations.
   a. Use illustrations from the book.
   b. Use child-drawn illustrations.
      1) book form
      2) TV scroll
   c. After the child draws a scene from the story, he may wish to dictate a description to the teacher.
   d. Children make drawings for the *Class Sequence Book* (See Chapter 7).
5. Tape-recorder.
   a. Child tells story to tape recorder and plays it for a friend.
   b. Small group of children retell the story sequentially and record.
C. After the initial retelling experience, the child should be encouraged to alter the original story slightly by:
   1. adding other characters (The Three Pigs visit The Three Bears)
   2. interchanging characters. (Goldilocks visits The Three Pigs)
   3. changing the setting. (The Three Bears in the city.)
   4. changing the personality of a character. (The Three Bears are very happy that Goldilocks came to visit).
   5. Changing the ending of the story. (Goldilocks returns with presents for the bears.)
D. After enjoying *Goldilocks and the Three Bears* the children can compare:
   1. several versions of the classic orally and in written form.
   2. The Three Bears to other bear books.

III. Using Book Illustrations.
   A. Child participates in discussion concerning the various types of illustrations and methods used to produce them.
      1. Appearance of the bears; realistic or Teddy
      2. Type of clothing, if any
      3. Appearance of the cottage
      4. Furniture in the cottage

5. Appearance of Goldilocks.
6. Types of illustrations.
    a. watercolor
    b. collage
    c. photographs
B. Children should be encouraged to express preferences. Emphasis should be placed on the use of descriptive words.

IV. Vocabulary.
A. Quality children's literature is an excellent source for enriching vocabulary.
B. Hearing the story is one way of increasing the child's vocabulary.
C. Special words may be emphasized:
    1. Before the story emphasize "cottage."
    2. During the story emphasize "porridge," "wee," "mischief," "snuggled."
    3. After the story emphasize "great big voice," "gruff voice."
D. Children could suggest synonyms for selected words as the story is retold.
E. Bear Words (See Chapter 3)

V. Written Responses.
A. Talking about books and writing down what has been said is an excellent way to make reading meaningful.
B. The teacher can write down many things about a book after it has been read and discussed.
    1. Names and descriptions of characters.
        a. "little small wee baby bear"
        b. "great big bear"
    2. Names and descriptions of settings.
        a. "pretty little house"
        b. "middle of the woods"
    3. Sequence of events (see *Class Sequence Book,* Chapter 7).
        a. cooking porridge
        b. walk in the forest
        c. Goldilocks' arrival
        d. tasting, sitting, sleeping
        e. bears return
    4. Spontaneous descriptions for children's pictures.

VI. Art Responses.
A. Materials should be available so that the child feels free to respond artistically to the story.
B. Possible artistic responses:
    1. Children model the three bears out of clay.
    2. Children contribute to Walk in the Woods mural which shows what the bears saw on their walk.

3. Children make crayon bear portraits.
4. After comparing the illustrations of four versions of *Goldilocks and the Three Bears*, children experiment with four types of media to create a bear. Consider using crayon, tempera, pencil and watercolor.

VII Food Experiences and Books.
  A. Occasionally a book lends itself well to specific food experiences.
    1. Cooking porridge or oatmeal.
    2. Making Peanut Butter Playdough Bears (see Chapter 7)
    3. Making Ginger Bears (See Chapter 7)
  B. Children can help prepare these snacks.

——— Bear Book Activities ———

Browne, Anthony. *Bear Hunt.* Atheneum, 1980.
SUMMARY: Hunters after a bear are consistently outwitted as Bear takes his pencil and draws his way out of the situation.
  1. RETELL STORY
      Objective: Child listens to story and retells it.
  2. LISTEN AND PREDICT
      Objective: Child listens to story and predicts bear's drawings.
  3. HIDDEN PICTURES
      Objective: Child searches for hidden pictures in the illustrations.
  4. COMPARE
      Objective: After hearing both stories, child compares methods used to solve problems.
      Materials: *Harold and the Purple Crayon*
  5. TRAP DRAW
      Objective: Child draws other possible traps and bear's drawing of escape.
      Materials: crayons, paper
  6. "BEAR HUNT"
      Objective: Child participates in large group "Bear Hunt."
      Procedure: Using the activity, "Let's Go On A Bear Hunt," as basis, teacher takes children on an imaginary bear hunt. Teacher emphasizes movement, memory, and group participation.

Douglas, Barbara. *Good As New.* Illustrated by Patience Brewster. Lothrop, Lee & Shepard, 1982.
SUMMARY: When Grady's young cousin ruins his Teddy Bear, Grandpa promises to fix the toy.
  1. FELT STORY
      Objective: Child retells the story using felt characters.
      Materials: Felt pictures representing bear, Grandpa, and boys. Felt board.

2. COPING
   Objective: Child describes how each of the characters was frustrated and how each coped with his frustration.
3. FAMILY ROLE DISCUSSION
   Objective: Child discusses family roles. Teacher emphasizes generations, extended family, and sex-role responsibilities.
4. RECYCLE A BEAR
   Objective: Child tells how to recycle a bear. Teacher may choose to record the list.

Freeman, Don. *Corduroy.* Viking, 1968.
SUMMARY: Corduroy, a small bear who lives in a toy department, wants someone to take him home. His meeting with Lisa, adventures in the store, and later purchase by Lisa, offer a gentle story.
1. RETELL STORY
   Objective: Child retells the story using the illustrations. Teacher emphasizes sequencing and vocabulary development (apartment, escalator, department).
2. TOUCH FABRIC
   Objective: Child touches each sample fabric and describes similarities and differences in the feel of each.
   Materials: Swatches of different types of materials (e.g., corduroy, velvet, satin, denim, etc.)
3. MY OWN CORDUROY
   Objective: Child draws, cuts out, and retells own version of *Corduroy.*
   Materials: paper, crayons, catalog, large paper
   Procedure: Make a paper corduroy bear. Search through catalogs for pictures of items found in a department store, including toys and beds. Cut out the pictures and glue them on paper. Retell the story, moving his own Corduroy to the appropriate department in the "store."
4. LET'S TALK MONEY
   Objective: Child discusses basic economic issues, such as family financial problems, earnings and savings of children, etc. Could lead to a trip to a local department store.

Freeman, Don. *A Pocket for Corduroy.* Viking, 1978.
SUMMARY: Searching for a pocket, Corduroy becomes separated from Lisa at a laundromat. His adventures, before being reunited with Lisa, are both amusing and touching.
1. LISA'S GROWTH
   Objective: Recalling Freeman's *Corduroy,* child observes illustrations to find things which indicate a passage of time between

both stories (e. g., Lisa's growth, Mother's appearance changes).
Materials: *Corduroy*

2. RETELL STORY
Objective: Child retells the story using illustrations as a clue.
Teacher emphasizes vocabulary development and sequencing.

3. PRECIOUS POCKET
Objective: Child makes a pocket out of construction paper. Cut out magazine pictures of "precious" things and place them in the pocket. Alternative: Draw and color "precious" items.
Materials: Construction paper, magazines, crayons, scissors, glue

4. WHAT'S IN THE POCKET?
Objective: Child sees items and is able to describe them once they are hidden.
Materials: large cloth pocket or multi-pocket shoe bag, assortment of items commonly carried in pockets (e. g., money, hanky, tissue, comb, small toys, pocket watch, etc.)
Procedures: Teacher displays and names a set of objects. Teacher then places items in pocket. Take turns naming items. As each item is named, remove it from the pocket. Teacher emphasizes visual recall and vocabulary.

5. COMPARE THREE STORIES
Objective: Child compares three stories.
Materials: Ormandroyd's *Theodore*, Skorpen's *Charles*.

Kantrowitz, Mildred. *Willy Bear.* Illustrated by Nancy Winslow Parker. New York: Four Winds, 1976.
SUMMARY: On the eve of his first day at school, a child projects some of his uneasiness onto his Teddy Bear, Willy.

1. RETELLS STORY
Objective: Child listens to story and retells it in correct sequence.

2. WILLY'S FEARS
Objective: Child participates in a discussion concerning who is really afraid.

3. THINGS WE FEAR
Objective: Child participates in the development of a list of fears of the boy and compares these fears with others that children might know.
Materials: chart paper, markers

Murphy, Jill. *Peace at Last.* Dial, 1980.
SUMMARY: Mr. Bear spends the night searching for enough peace and quiet to go to sleep.
1. RETELLING
    Objective: Child listens to the story and retells it.
    Materials: puppets or three real teddy bears
    Procedure: Use puppets or three bears to retell story and encourage audience to participate in sound effects
2. DISCUSSING
    Objective: Discuss night sounds
    Materials: chart paper, marker
    Procedure: List night sounds suggested by the children. After the list is developed, categorize sounds: loud, soft, scary, special sounds, "normal."
3. COMPOSING
    Objective: Child develops story variations.
    Procedure: As a class book extend the story using sounds in the classroom that might be disturbing, (e.g. noisy children, bells, sweeper). Individuals could rewrite the story including their own families and sounds at their own house.
4. SOUND COLLAGE
    Objective: Child makes a sound collage by cutting and gluing magazine pictures of things that make sounds.
    Materials: magazines, glue or paste, large construction paper

Ormondroyd, Edward. *Theodore.* Illustrated by Frank Larrecq. Parnassus, 1966.
SUMMARY: Theodore knew he was loved even though Lucy sometimes forgot him and was careless.
1. FELT STORY
    Objective: Child retells the story using the flannel board and cutouts. Teacher emphasizes correct sequence and vocabulary development (such as basement, bedroom).
    Materials: Flannel board, magazine or catalog cut-outs backed with sandpaper or felt, to illustrate the story.
2. NEW WORDS
    Objective: Child participates in a discussion concerning unfamiliar vocabulary (e.g., "smudgy," "careless," "fainted").
3. REBUS STORY
    Objective: Child retells story as teacher writes it in rebus style (picture) on chalkboard or chart paper.
    Materials: chalkboard or chart paper.
4. FAMILY ROLES
    Objective: child participates in discussion concerning family roles in the home.

Procedure: Compare real family member roles and responsibilities with those in the story (in particular Father's ineptness with the laundry).

5. COMPARING FRIENDS

Objective: Child compares the two story lines (e. g., laundromat experiences, relationships between Theodore and Lucy, Corduroy and Lisa, etc.).

Pinkwater, Manus. *Bear's Picture.* Holt, Rhinehart & Winston, 1972.

SUMMARY: Bear sat down to paint a picture. Two gentlemen came along and told him that bears never painted pictures and that his painting didn't look like anything to them. Bear informs them that it is *his* painting and therefore needs to please only *him.*

1. RETELL STORY

Objective: Child listens to story and retells it in sequence.

2. THE PICTURE

Objective: Child listens to story and interprets bear's picture.

3. STUDY A PRINT

Objective: Child describes, interprets and evaluates prints.

4. PAINTING BY CHOICE

Objective: Child paints what pleases him. Perhaps comments about other children's paintings, but only in positive statements.

Rockwell, Anne. *Albert B. Cub and Zebra.* Crowell, 1977.

SUMMARY: Albert B. Cub searches through the alphabet and around the world for his missing friend Zebra. This is a wordless picture book with a story at the end for additional experience.

1. TELL A STORY

Objective: Child describes the pictures and tells what might be happening. Locate Albert B. Cub in each picture.

2. NAME A LETTER

Objective: Child participates in identifying the letters featured on each page.

3. NAME AN OBJECT

Objective: Child identifies items in the picture that begin with the letter featured on the page.

4. DECORATE A LETTER

Objective: After choosing large letter cut-outs, child finds and cuts out magazine pictures starting with the chosen letters. Child glues them on the letter, creating a letter montage.

Alternate: Draw and color appropriate pictures on their letters.

Materials: large letters cut from construction paper, scissors, glue or paste, magazine pictures.

5. NEW WORDS

   Objective: After listening to the story at the end of the book, child participates in a discussion identifying and discussing unfamiliar words.

Waber, Bernard. *Ira Sleeps Over.* Houghton-Mifflin, 1972.
SUMMARY: For the first time in his life, Ira is invited to sleep at a friend's house. His excitement is tempered somewhat by his sister's teasing concerning taking his Teddy Bear along. His decision not to take the bear, and how that decision is later changed, provides an entertaining and realistic portrayal of a young boy's experiences.

1. RETELL STORY

   Objective: Child retells the story using illustrations as clues. Teacher emphasizes vocabulary development and sequence.

2. SECURITY

   Objective: Using the book as a foundation, child participates in discussions about such issues as: security symbols, sibling relationships (teasing, etc.) and similar real-life situations and experiences.

Wildsmith, Brian. *The Lazy Bear.* New York: Franklin Watts, 1974.
SUMMARY: When the bear found the woodcutter's wagon, he invited his friends to share the fun. His idea of fun didn't necessarily agree with the opinions of his friends. How they convinced the bear what sharing really means makes this a delightful and thought-provoking book.

1. RETELL STORY

   Objective: Using the illustrations, child retells the story. Teacher emphasizes vocabulary and sequencing.

2. SHARING

   Objective: Using the story as a foundation, child participates in discussion about sharing and friendship.

3. PAINTING BY CHOICE

   Objective: Child participates in a discussion about Wildsmith's vivid illustrations. Experiment and explore the art media using bright or flourescent paints.
   Materials: Tempera paints, paper, paint brushes

4. COMPARE THE PICTURES

   Objective: Using these (or other) books, child observes the different types of illustrations and develops some ideas as to what methods the artists used to achieve the effect.

Felt Board

The felt board or flannel board is another visual approach to children's literature. Many children's books can be adapted to this media. See suggestions in Chapter 2.

Children usually find felt board materials irresistable and will readily use the materials to retell the stories on their own.

The following story is designed specifically for the felt board. Following the story are patterns for the characters and directions for their construction.

The First Teddy Bear
Flannel Board Story

Once upon a time there was a Great Toy Maker who created all kinds of toys to please boys and girls. Each day the Toy Maker worked on a new toy. As the toy was finished, it gave him great joy. One day, as he sat at his work bench, he picked up some soft brown fur. "This would make a lovely toy," he said. So he made a fat chubby body of soft brown fur. (Put body on the flannel board).

Next he made two long, brown, furry legs. (Add the legs to the body on the flannel board).

Then the Toy Maker made two short, brown, furry arms. (Put the arms on the figure taking form on the flannel board).

Lastly, he added a little tan paw to each arm and leg. (Add the paws to the arms).

Then the Toy Maker stepped back to see what he had made. Something was missing. "Of course, the head!" he said. And the Toy Maker thought "What sort of a head should I give this toy?" He finally thought out loud. "Perhaps one like I used on the Scotty dog would do." So he put it on the fat, furry body. (Put the Scotty dog head on the flannel board figure).

As he stood back to look at his toy, he shook his head, "No, that Scotty's head won't do at all!" He tried a horse's head on the furry body. (Put the horse's head on the figure).

He still wasn't satisfied. Next, he tried an elephant's head. (Put the elephant's head on the figure).

He knew, as he stepped back and considered the toy, that the elephant's head wouldn't do either. It just didn't look right on that fat brown body. Then he tried a rooster's head. (Put the rooster's head on the figure).

And a pig's head. (Put the pig's head on the figure).

Then he said, "It is very plain to see that this new toy must have his own special head." So he made a large furry, brown ball, and on this he put

a black, shiny nose,
two black eyes and,
a round cherry-red mouth.

Last of all, he added: two brown, furry ears!

"Now I think that will be all!" said the Toy Maker. As he stepped back to look at his newest toy, he smiled; then broke into a laugh! He laughed and laughed, until the tears spilled out of his eyes and fell down over his cheeks. This was a happy day for the Great Toy Maker, for he had just made the very First Teddy Bear!

– Anonymous

Todd, Vivian. *The Aide in Early Childhood Education*, New York: Macmillan, 1973, pp. 191 – 193.

Retell *The First Teddy Bear.*

MATERIALS
assorted felt or pellon
- brown (bear) (horse)
- tan (bear paws)
- gray (elephant)
- black (Scotty)
- pink (pig)
- white, red (rooster)
- markers
- scissors

CONSTRUCTION
Trace and cut pattern pieces from felt or pellon. Add features with markers.

PLAY
After hearing *The First Teddy Bear,* the child retells the story.

Variations:
- Child adds possible character heads.
- Child changes main character to an animal, his mother, himself.
- Child develops a new story: *The First Clown, The First Cookie Maker,* etc.

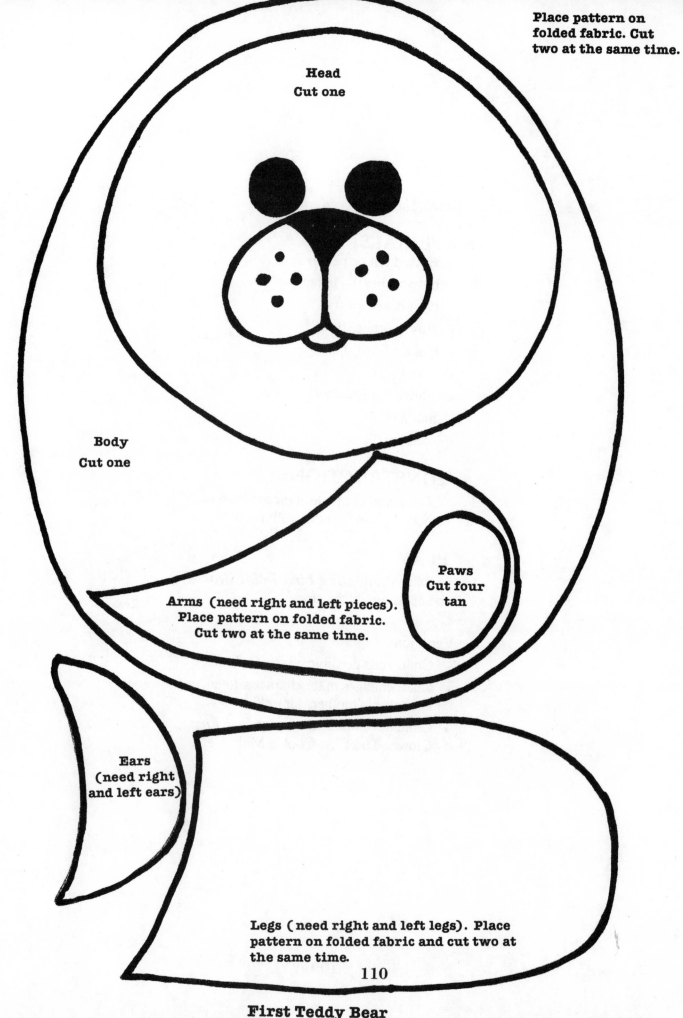

Place pattern on folded fabric. Cut two at the same time.

Head
Cut one

Body
Cut one

Paws
Cut four
tan

Arms (need right and left pieces).
Place pattern on folded fabric.
Cut two at the same time.

Ears
(need right
and left ears)

Legs (need right and left legs). Place
pattern on folded fabric and cut two at
the same time.

110

First Teddy Bear

Horse

Dog

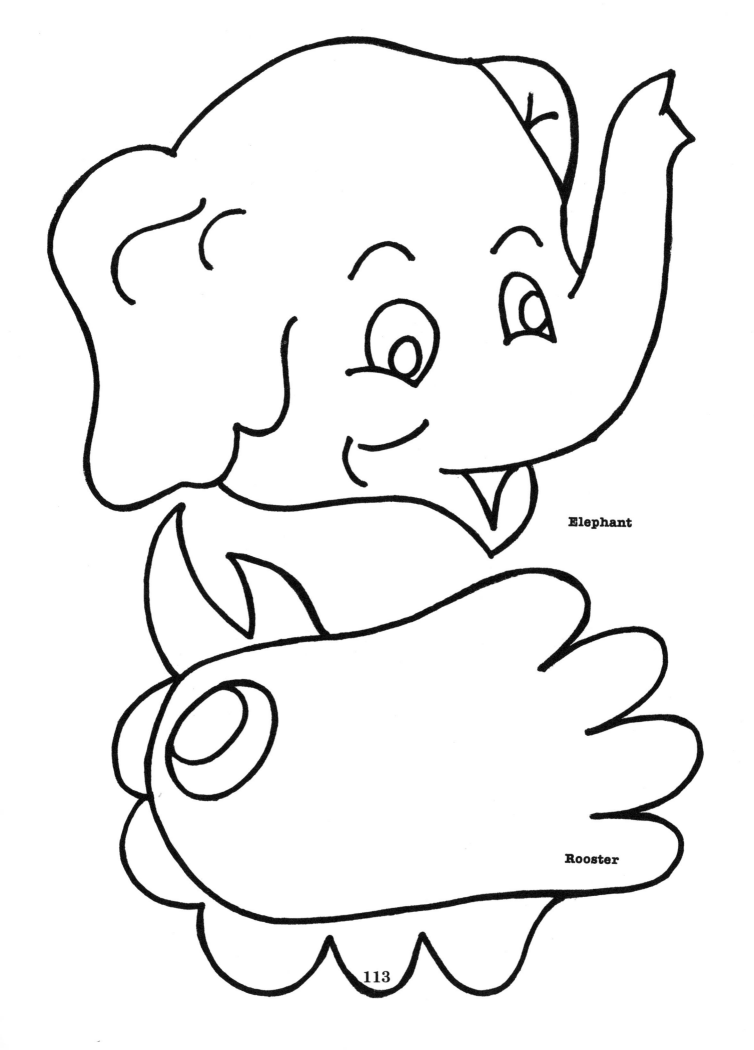

Elephant

Rooster

113

Pig

Selected Bibliography

Alexander, Martha. *Blackboard Bear*. Dial, 1969. When a little boy has a big bear, being little doesn't matter quite so much.

Alexander, Martha. *I Am Sure Glad to See You, Blackboard Bear*. Dial, 1976. Little Anthony's bear is immensely helpful when he has to deal with children who are teasing, selfish or bullying.

Alexander, Martha. *We're In Big Trouble, Blackboard Bear*. Dial, 1980. Anthony's bear learns a hard lesson about leaving other people's things alone.

Asch, Frank. *Bread and Honey*. Parents Magazine, 1981. Ben paints a picture of his mother with a little help from Owl, Rabbit, Alligator, Elephant, Lion, and Giraffe.

Asch, Frank. *Popcorn*. Parents Magazine. 1979. Sam Bear invites his friends to an impromptu Halloween party and asks them to bring a treat. (Follow-up; Popping corn.)

Binzen, Bill. *Alfred Goes Flying*. Doubleday, 1976. Alfred and his cousin Huckleberry construct a miniature plane to carry them to Goose Lake for a vacation.

Binzen, Bill. *Alfred Goes House Hunting*. Doubleday, 1974. Spring is in the air and Alfred decides to move outdoors for the summer. Finding a home is not as easy as it sounds.

Binzen, Bill. *Alfred The Little Bear*. Doubleday, 1970. Alfred, sad and bored, decides to go exploring in the woods. He encounters some surprises, then becomes frightened when it becomes dark and windy and he hears spooky noises.

Browne, Anthony. *Bear Hunt*. Atheneum, 1980. Hunters after a bear are consistently outwitted as Bear takes his pencil and draws his way out of the situation.

Brustlein, Janice. *Little Bear Learns to Read the Cookbook*. Illustrated by Mariana. Lothrop, Lee & Shepard, 1969. Little Bear doesn't feel he can do anything— except make pancakes. Then the Baker gives him a cookbook and it starts him on the new adventure of learning how to read. Only in this way can he learn how to make chocolate cake in fifty different varieties.

Brustlein, Janice. *Little Bear Marches in the St. Patrick's Day Parade*. Ilustrated by Mariana. Lothrop, Lee & Shepard, 1967. Little Bear and his magic umbrella stop the rain and save the St. Patrick's Day Parade.

Brustlein, Janice. *Little Bear's Thanksgiving Party*. Illustrated by Mariana. Lothrop, Lee & Shepard, 1967. Little Bear is invited to a Thanksgiving dinner. Worried that he might be asleep by then, his friends agree to make sure he gets to the dinner. Although he does fall asleep, the magic words, "pumpkin pie," wake him up quickly.

Davidson, Amanda. *Teddy's First Christmas*. Holt, Rinehart & Winston, 1982. A Teddy Bear's adventures on Christmas Eve.

Dionetti, Michelle. *The Day Eli Went Looking for Bear*. Illustrated by Joyce Dos Santos. Addison-Wesley, 1980. On a cold winter day Eli and his dog go into the woods to catch a bear.

Douglas, Barbara. *Good As New.* Illustrated by Patience Brewer. Lothrop, Lee & Shepard, 1982. When Grady's young cousin ruins his Teddy Bear, Grandpa promises to fix the toy.

Flack, Marjorie. *Ask Mr. Bear.* Macmillan, 1932. The little boy is hunting for a present for his mother. He asks all the animals, but nothing seems to be the right present until he asks Mr. Bear.

Flory, Jane. *The Bear on the Doorstep.* Illustrated by Carolyn Croll. Houghton-Mifflin, 1980. Young bear is adored by the rabbits who find him on their doorstep and adopt him, but his size soon becomes a problem in their crowded little house.

Freeman, Don. *Corduroy.* Viking, 1968. Corduroy, a small bear who lives in a toy department, wants someone to take him home. His meeting with Lisa, adventures in the store, and later purchase by Lisa, offer a gentle story.

Freeman, Don. *A Pocket for Corduroy.* Viking, 1978. Searching for a pocket, Corduroy becomes separated from Lisa at the laundromat.

Freschet, Berniece. *Black Bear Baby.* Illustrated by J. Arnosky. Putnam, 1981. Describes the first months of the life of Bear Baby and his sister. Includes factual material and picture of a bear paw print.

Galdone, Paul. *The Three Bears.* Seabury Press, 1972. Traditional story.

Gordon, Margaret. *Wilberforce Goes on a Picnic.* Morrow, 1982. Brief text and illustrations depict activities from sunrise to sunset the day before Wilberforce and his family go on a picnic.

Gretz, Susanna. *Teddybears ABC.* Follett, 1975. Teddy Bears go through an active alphabet.

Guilfoile, E. *Nobody Listens to Andrew.* Follett, 1957. Nobody listens when Andrew tries to tell them there is a bear in his bed.

Hague, Kathleen. *Alphabears. An ABC Book.* Illustrated by Michael Hague. Holt, Rinehart and Winston, 1984 Introduces a bear for each letter of the alphabet and describes its qualities in rhyme.

Harlow, Joan Hiatt, *Shadow Bear.* Illustrated by J. Arnosky, Doubleday, 1981. George, an Eskimo boy, and Tarrack, a polar bear cub, discover new meanings about the stories told to them about "giant" hunters and "giant" polar bears.

Hayes, Geoffrey. *Bear By Himself.* Harper & Row, 1976. A bear enjoys his moments alone.

Isenberg, Barbara, and Susan Wolf. *The Adventures of Albert, the Running Bear.* Illustrated by Dick Gackenback. Clarion, 1982. Following his escape from the zoo, Albert Bear encounters a series of mishaps and finally finds himself running in a marathon.

Janice. See Brustlein, Janice.

Kantrowitz, Mildred. *Willy Bear.* Illustrated by Nancy Parker. Four Winds, 1976. On the eve of his first day at school, a child projects some of his uneasiness onto his Teddy Bear, Willy.

Kennedy, Jimmy. *The Teddy Bears' Picnic.* Illustrated by Alexandra Day. LaJolla. Green Tiger Press, 1983. Elaborate illustrations detail the 1907 song of the picnic in the woods. (Record)

Krauss, Ruth, *Bears.* Illustrated by Phyllis Rowand. Harper, Row, 1948.

Bears, bears, bears, bears. Under chairs. . ... Washing hairs. . . This book is filled with funny bears in funny places.

Mack, Stan. *Ten Bears in My Bed*. Pantheon, 1974. A goodnight countdown book. Similar to the song/story, "Roll Over," each bear exits the room in a different movement pattern: fly, gallop, roar, skate, chug, jump, bounce, pedal, tootle and rumble.

Martin, Bill, Jr. *Brown Bear, Brown Bear, What Do You See?* Illustrated by Eric Carle. Holt, Rinehart, and Winston, 1967. Brown Bear leads the children through a story filled with different colors and animals. (Patterned language)

McCloskey, Robert. *Blueberries for Sal*. Viking, 1948. A small girl and a small bear accompany their mothers on a hunt for blueberries.

McPhail, David. *Bear's Toothache*. Little, Brown, 1972. A young boy helps a bear with a toothache — creating a marvelous commotion and a huge amount of fun.

McPhail, David. *Fix-It*. Dutton, 1984. It is when the Fix-it man is trying to repair the television and her parents are trying to entertain her that Emma becomes so interested in reading, she no long cares about TV.

Minarik, Else. H. *A Kiss for Little Bear*. Illustrated by M. Sendak. Harper & Row, 1968. Little Bear draws a picture and sends it to his Grandmother. She sends a kiss back to him via the other animals.

Morris, T. *Goodnight, Dear Monster!* Random House, A.A. Knopf, 1980. A little girl, her Teddy Bear, and a bedtime monster become friends.

Murphy, Jill. *Peace at Last*. Dial, 1980. Mr. Bear spends the night searching for enough peace and quiet to go to sleep.

Myers, Bernice. *Not This Bear*. Four Winds, 1969. Dressed in a furry hat and coat, little Herman looks just like a bear. That's exactly what a bear thinks as bear and boy pass in the woods.

Nakatani, Chiyoko. *My Teddy Bear*. Thomas Y. Crowell, 1975. A Teddy Bear is to play with , to love, to fight with, and to sleep with — in other words, it is a small child's very best friend.

Ormondroyd, Edward. *Theodore*. Illustrated by John Larrecq. Parnassus, 1966. Theodore knew he was loved even though Lucy sometimes forgot him and was careless.

Ormondroyd, Edward. *Theodore's Rival*. Illustrated by John Larrecq. Parnassus, 1971. Theodore's security is threatened when Lucy receives a panda for her birthday.

Parker, Nancy Winslow. *The Ordeal of Bryon B. Blackbear*. Dodd & Mead, 1979. A world-famous scientist's study of a hibernating bear produces surprising results.

Pinkwater, Manus. *Bear's Picture*. Holt, Rinehart & Winston, 1972. Bear sat down to paint a picture. Two gentlemen came along and told him that bears never paint pictures and that his painting didn't look like anything to them. Bear informed them that it's his painting and therefore needs to please only him.

Pluckrose, Henry, Consultant Ed. *Bears*. Illustrated by Richard Orr. Gloucester, 1979. Factual book describing bears of the world, their characteristics, habitat and feeding.

Rockwell, Anne. *Albert B. Cub and Zebra.* Thomas Y. Crowell, 1977. Albert B. Cub searches through the alphabet and around the world for his missing friend, Zebra. This is a wordless picture book with a story at the end for additional experience.

Rockwell, Anne. *First Comes Spring.* Thomas Y. Crowell, 1985. Bear Child notices that the clothes he wears, the things everyone does at work and play, and the other parts of his world all change with the seasons.

Scott, Evelyn. *The Fourteen Bears in Summer and Winter.* Illustrated by Virginia Parsons. Golden, 1972. A delightfully illustrated story of Mother and Daddy Bear and their 12 children.

Sharmat, Marjorie W. *I'm Terrific.* Illustrated by Kay Chorao. Holiday House, 1977. Jason Bear thinks he's terrific and even awards himself gold stars for superior performance in his chores. His friends don't like to be around him.

Siewert, Margaret and Kathleen Savage. *Bear Hunt.* Illustrated by Leonard Shortall. Prentice-Hall, 1976. In this rendition of a children's game, a Teddy Bear on a bear hunt crosses rivers, bridges, cliffs, and swamps, meets the real bear, and rushes home again.

Skorpen, Liesel Moak. *Charles.* Illustrated by M. Alexander. Harper & Row, 1971. Charles was a sad and lonely bear in the toy shop who didn't belong to anyone and no one belonged to him. Charles was given as a gift to a little girl who didn't understand him. He was more unhappy than ever until a little boy changed his life.

Turkle, B. *Deep In The Forest.* Dutton, 1976. A curious bear explores a cabin in the forest with disastrous results. (Wordless reverse story of the traditional, *Three Bears.*).

Virin, Anna. *Elsa's Bears Learn to Paint.* Harvey House, 1974. Elsa's bears help paint each other.

Waber, Bernard. *Ira Sleeps Over.* Houghton-Mifflin, 1972. For the first time in his life, Ira is invited to sleep over at a friend's house. Should he take his Teddy or not take him becomes a difficult decision.

Watanabe, Shigeo. *How Do I Put It On?* Illustrated by Y. Ohtomo. Philomel, 1977. A bear demonstrates the right and wrong ways to put on shirt, pants, cap and shoes.

Wild, Robin and Jocelyn. *The Bear's ABC Book.* Lippincott, 1977. Three delightful bears sort through a junk pile and find everything from an ax to a zebra.

Wildsmith, Brian. *The Lazy Bear.* Franklin Watts, 1974. When the bear found the woodcutter's wagon, he invited his friends to share the fun. His idea of fun didn't necessarily agree with the opinion of his friends. How they convinced the bear what sharing really means makes this a delightful and thought-provoking book.

Worthington, Phoebe and Joan. *Teddy Bear Gardener.* London: Warne, 1983. Detailed description of a gardener's day.

Zalben, Jane Breskin. *A Perfect Nose for Ralph.* Illustrated by John Wallner. Philomel, 1980. When his panda's fuzzy black nose fell off and got lost, a little boy decided to find a perfect nose with which to replace it.

Chapter Four

ACTIVITIES FOR MATHEMATICS

Mathematics Overview

This chapter includes activities which develop these mathematical skills:

classification and matching

numeral/number recognition

observation

patterning recognition/extension

size seriation

comparison

Many of the activities which develop visual discrimination are also appropriate for language arts.

Bear Concentration

Bear Poke

Bear Twins

Belly Button Bear

Button Color Sort

Color Bear Patterning

Domino Bear

Echo Bear

Face Lace

Honey Hunt

Hungry Bear

Mama Bear

Matrix

Number Bears

Numeral Dot Bear

Pocket Patterns

Sequence Bears

Teddy Bear Counters

Texture Bears

Three Bears' House

Bear Concentration

Child matches bears.

MATERIALS

- white poster board
- colored poster board (8 basic colors)
- scissors
- Laminator or Contact paper
- markers

CONSTRUCTION

Trace and cut 33 bears. Make four out of each of the eight basic colors. Leave one bear white. Using black marker, outline bears and draw facial features. Laminate or cover bears with Contact.

PLAY

All bears are placed face down in rows on playing surface. First player turns over two bears. If the colors match, player keeps that pair and continues turning over two cards at a time until they do not match. If the colors do not match, the player turns the bears face down in their original position. The second player continues the game in the same manner. Play continues until all pairs are matched. Player with the most pairs can be the winner — but it is not necessary to declare a "winner."

Bear Concentration

Child matches number with numeral by poking through the hole under the numeral.

MATERIALS

- 4-inch by 6-inch unruled index cards (20 +)
- markers
- press apply labels (approx. 1 inch by 1½ inch)
- single hold punch
- pencil with unused eraser
- black ink stamp pad
- golf tees (for poking)
- Laminator or Contact paper

CONSTRUCTION

Trace or duplicate bears on index cards. Color bears with markers. Use pencil eraser as a rubber stamp. Put a different number of dots on each label using domino dot patterns, 1 – 9. (See Domino Bears, Chapter 4). Mount labels as shown. Near the lower edge of the card, punch three holes as indicated. Write numerals above each hole, with only one numeral being the correct choice. On the back side of the card, draw a circle around the hole under the correct number. Laminate or Contact. Punch holes.

Variations: Match small pictures with beginning letters or match capital letters and lowercase letters.

Bear Poke

122

Child matches bears.

MATERIALS

- variety of small print wallpaper samples, contact paper, or gift wrapping (10 – 15)
- bear pattern
- 3-inch by 6-inch white posterboard (10 – 15)
- rubber cement
- Contact paper or Laminator

CONSTRUCTION

Using the bear pattern, trace and cut out two from each variety of paper. Use rubber cement to attach the bears to the posterboard. Laminate or Contact. Puzzle each rectangle uniquely.

Variations:

1. Match lowercase letters
2. Match upper and lower case letters.
3. Match phone numbers (write number on   or under patterned bear)
4. Match numbers.

Bear Twins

123

Belly Button Bear

Child matches bears by smell.

MATERIALS

- bear pattern (see Bear Concentration, Chapter 4)
- posterboard
- scissors
- marker (black)
- sniff stickers, press apply; ten pairs (available commercially)
- Laminator or Contact paper

CONSTRUCTION

1. Trace pattern and make 20 posterboard bears.
2. Add facial and body lines with black marker.
3. Cut out bears
4. Laminate or cover bears with Contact paper.
5. Attach sniff stickers to the navel areas of bears. Make two bears with each sticker.

PLAY

Child closes eyes, and attempts to match bears by smelling stickers.

Button Color Sort

Child sorts buttons by color.

MATERIALS

- 8 or 9 different colors of yarn
- 7-inch by 7-inch pieces of white tag
- glue
- buttons of different sizes, shapes and colors
- scissors

CONSTRUCTION

Trace one bear head onto each piece of tag board. Glue a colored piece of yarn to outline each bear head.

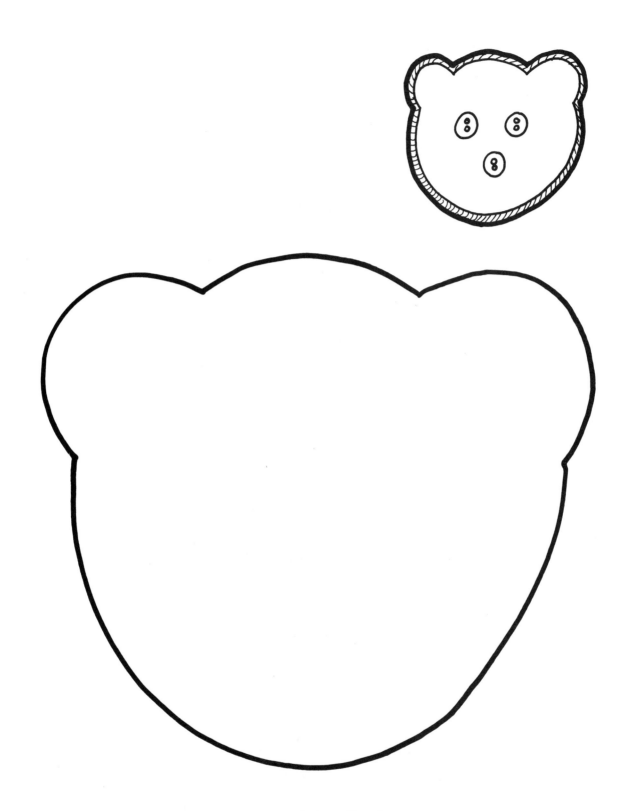

Button Color Sort

Color Bear Patterning

Child will copy and/or extend color patterns.

MATERIALS

- oak tag sentence strips or oak tag strips (3 inches x 24 inches)
- circle stickers (approx. ¾ inch) red, yellow, blue, green
- Teddy Bear Counters (Milton Bradley)
- Laminator or Contact paper

CONSTRUCTION

Use colored circles to begin a color pattern at the left edge of the sentence strip. Vary the patterns from simple to complex. Vary the number of repetitions shown. Suggested types are:

Two color:
blue, green; blue, green . . .
or green, green, blue; green, green, blue . . .
or blue, blue, green; blue, blue, green...

Three color:
red, blue, yellow; red, blue, yellow...
or red, red, blue, yellow; red, red, red, blue, yellow . . .
or blue, blue, red, red, green, green...
or red, blue, blue, green; red, blue, blue, green . . .

Four color:
red, yellow, blue, green; red, yellow, blue, green . . .

Laminate or cover with Contact paper as desired.

PLAY

Child places appropriate color of bear of each pattern circle, then uses color bears to extend the pattern to the end of the sentence strip.

Domino Bears (Double Six)

Child matches number sets on dominoes.

MATERIALS

- poster board or 14 ply cardboard (28 pieces, 3-inches by 6-inches)
- small rubber stamp bear (available commercially)
- black ink stamp pad
- paper cutter
- bear-colored markers (brown, ginger, yellow, etc.)
- black wide tip marker
- ruler
- Laminator or Contact paper

CONSTRUCTION

Cut cardboard into 2" x 4" rectangles. Use black marker to draw a line dividing each card in half. Using bear stamp and ink pad, reproduce domino set pattern on cards. Color bears. Laminate or cover with Contact as desired.

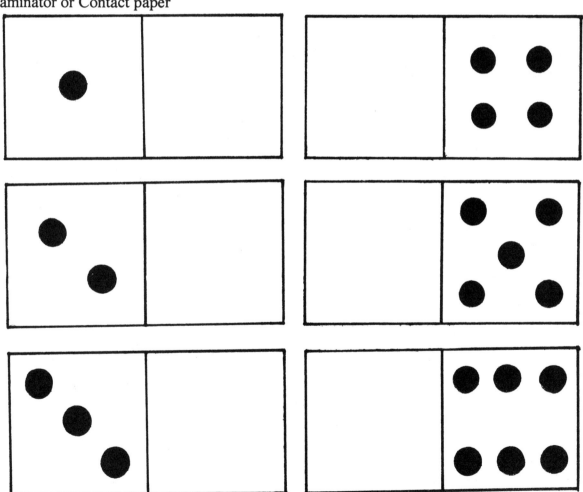

Echo Bear

Child hears and repeats a series of words.

MATERIALS
- construction paper (assorted colors)
- white rectangular labels (1" x 3")
- scissors
- markers
- Laminator or Contact paper

CONSTRUCTION
Trace 40 bears on construction paper. With black marking pen, outline each bear and draw a face. On each label, write a sequence of numbers (3 5 8 2), letters (p f t), or draw pictures or shapes. Vary the number of items in a sequence (from two to five) to produce various levels of difficulty. Attach a label to each bear. Laminate or cover the bears with Contact. Cut out bears.

PLAY
First child reads the sequence appearing on the bear. Second child orally repeats the sequence heard. If correct, the answering child keeps the bear for the duration of the game.

Echo Bear

Face Lace

Child matches identical bear faces.

MATERIALS

- posterboard or cardboard (9" x 12")
- paper drill (or ice pick)
- Face Lace illustration or Teddy Bear stickers
- three 27" shoestrings
- markers (six colors)
- Laminator or Contact paper

CONSTRUCTION

1. Place six different faces or stickers down the left side of the cardboard. Place the same six faces down the right side, but in a different order.
2. Use paper drill to make a hole next to each face.
3. To make the game self-checking, use markers to draw a different color of circle around each hole in the left column on game front.
4. On the back of the cardboard, color code each correct matching hole by drawing the corresponding colored circle.
5. Laminate or Contact the cardboard.
6. Repunch all the holes.
7. Cut each shoestring in half, knot the cut end and pull through the left holes from the back. Knot the string again on the front, as close as possible to the cardboard.

PLAY

Child matches faces by lacing the shoestring across the board and down through the proper hole. Self-check by comparing the colored circles.

Face Lace

EXPRESSION BEARS

Child identifies shapes and colors while playing game.

MATERIALS

- 2 Teddy Bear counters (Milton Bradley) different colors
- file folder (letter size, colored)
- markers (eight basic colors)
- practice cards (2" x 3" or 3" x 5") cut in half
- paw rubber stamp or stencil
- shape rubber stamp or stencil
- ink pad for rubber stamp
- pencil
- Laminator or Contact paper

CONSTRUCTION

1. Game Board. Reproduce paw print pattern as shown. (Make stencil by cutting a similar print in a small margarine tub lid.) Be sure you make the path follow the left-right, top-bottom progression. Add drawing of bear and honey pot at the end of the path or add a bear sticker and/or a honey pot drawn on a press-apply label. Draw light pencil lines for title. Print title. Erase lines. (Or, write title on press-apply label.)

2. Cards. Make shape outlines on cards using rubber stamps or stencils. Choose shapes according to the practice needs of students. Use markers to color the shapes the eight basic colors. Use marker to draw one or two paw prints under the shape on the cards. (The numerals 1 or 2 could be used instead.) Laminate or Contact as desired.

PLAY

In turn, the two players choose a card. If they can correctly identify the color and shape on the card, they move their marker bear the appropriate number of steps indicated on the card. If they are unable to identify either the color or shape, they remain in the same place. Child whose bear reaches the honeypot first is the winner.

Variation:
1. Put letters on the cards to practice letter recognition.
2. Put numerals on the cards to practice numeral recognition.

Honey Hunt

Child matches patterns.

MATERIALS
- brown poster board or brown marker and tag board
- white paper
- black marker
- rubber cement
- scissors
- Laminator or Contact paper

CONSTRUCTION

Cut ten pairs of bears from brown tag board. Draw in faces on all bears. Cut ten circles (stomachs) from white paper. On the white stomachs, draw simple patterns of shapes, letters or numbers. Cement one stomach onto each of ten bears.

Cut out a hole that matches the circle in each of the remaining ten bears. Laminate all bears or cover with Contact paper on both sides. On the see-through (empty) stomachs, trace corresponding patterns using permanent marker.

Hungry Bear

Mama Bear

Child demonstrates understanding of the concepts of more and less.

MATERIALS
- oak tag
- patterns for cards, four copies
- markers (if desired)
- scissors
- Laminator or Contact paper

CONSTRUCTION
Reproduce four sets of cards on tag. Color if desired. Laminate or Contact. Cut cards apart.

PLAY
Shuffle and deal the 28 cards. Each player places his cards face down. Each player turns his top card face up. The player whose card has the greater number of bears, or the Mama Bear takes the cards played and puts them aside. If cards match, players turn up another card. Winner has the most cards.

Variation: Could be played so that the card with the fewest bears wins the round.

Mama Bear

Child sorts cards.

MATERIALS

- markers
- oak tag or file folders
- copies of Matrix
- Laminator or Contact paper

CONSTRUCTION (One Copy)

Mount copy on oak tag or inside a file folder. Color as desired. (Suggestion: coloring all of Mama Bear's things blue makes the game easier.) Contact or laminate.

Variations:

1. Matching. Use two matrices, one cut into 12 cards, one not cut. Match cards to Matrix.
2. Sorting. Cut one Matrix into 12 cards. Mount the three bears at the top of a file folder. Make columns so child can sort bear possessions.
3. Three of a Kind. (For two or three children, cut four matrices and one "wild" card). Deal each child six cards. Put the rest of the deck into a "draw" pile. Turn one card face up. As players draw and discard, they work toward getting three of a kind, which they place in front, face up. Winner lays down all of his cards first.
4. Concentration. (Prepare two matrices, cut apart.) Turn all cards face down. Play to get a matching pair (as two baby bear bowls), or play to get the four things that go together.

Number Bears

Numeral Dot Bear

Child associates numeral with number set (1 – 6).

MATERIALS

- brown poster board
- circle sticker dots (white, ¾")
- black marker: medium point, fine point
- dice or one inch cube and clear nail polish
- small chips to cover circle sticker dots
- scissors
- Laminator or Contact paper

CONSTRUCTION

1. Bear. Enlarge pattern bear to 20". Cut. Use markers to outline bear and complete details of eyes, nose, mouth and ears. Draw a vertical line dividing the body into halves. Place white sticker dots on all parts of the bear except the head and face, making sure there are equal numbers of dots on each half of the bear. Use medium point marker to write the numerals 1 – 6 on the white circles. Laminate bear or cover with Contact as desired.
2. Dice. Put dots on the inch cube (Domino patterns, 1 – 6). Paint cube with clear nail polish.

PLAY (for two)

Each child, in turn, rolls the dice and covers one appropriate numeral dot on his side of the bear with a chip. If he rolls a number and all of those numerals on his side are covered, he loses that turn. The child who covers all of his numeral dots first is the winner.

142

Pocket Patterns

Child matches identical pattern designs.

MATERIALS

- file folder
- 6 – 8 library pockets (3" x 3") or Contact Pockets (Chapter 2)
- oak tag for bears
- wallpaper samples (small patterns)
- rubber cement
- bear pattern (see Illustration 74, Sequence Bears, Chapter 4)
- Contact cement
- markers
- ruler
- razor blade
- scissors
- Laminator or Contact paper

CONSTRUCTION

1. Folder. Draw light pencil lines on folder to indicate placement of pockets. Write title on inside and outside of folder, also on tab. Add a theme picture to outside of folder. Laminate or cover with Contact.
2. Pockets. Cut wallpaper samples into small squares. Attach to pockets with rubber cement. Laminate or cover pockets with Contact. Slit pocket open with razor blade. Attach pockets to laminated folder with Contact cement.
3. Bears. Trace and cut three oak tag bears for each pocket. Cover each bear with matching wallpaper. Use rubber cement. Laminate or Contact all bears.

PLAY

Child places bears in pockets with matching wallpaper.

Sequence Bears

Child arranges bears in order by size.

MATERIALS

- brown construction paper and tag or posterboard
- markers
- scissors
- rubber cement or dry mount tissue
- Laminator or Contact paper
- bear patterns

CONSTRUCTION

Trace and cut one bear of each size from posterboard or construction paper mounted on tag. Draw in face and other desired features. Laminate or cover with Contact. For self-checking, number the bears' backs 1 – 9, from smallest to largest.

Construction Variation:

1. Make bears from pellon or felt.
   2. Make construction paper sweaters for each bear by drawing around appropriate body parts.

PLAY

1. Child places bears in order by size.
2. Child places sweaters in order by size.
3. Child places dressed bears in order by size.

Sequence Bears 123

144

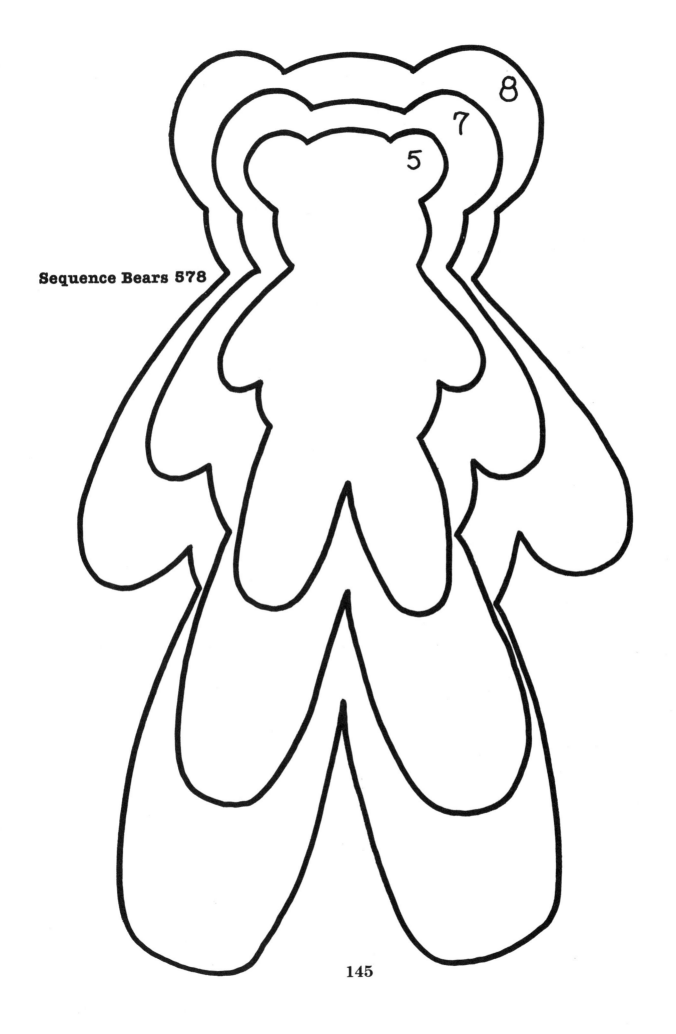

Sequence Bears 578

8

7

5

145

Teddy Bear Counters
(commercial product of Milton Bradley)

The Teddy Bear Counters are so appealing to young children that an immediate inter-action between child and bears is almost guaranteed. This versatility makes it possible to use them in a variety of activities, some of which are:

1. Bear in the Bottle
   Child drops Teddy Bear Counters into a bottle.

MATERIALS

- Teddy Bear Counters
- Plastic milk bottle (or any container having 2 – 3" opening)

PLAY

Child places bottle on floor and stands with his toes touching the bottle. Bear is held at tip of nose, then dropped. If more than one child is playing, each child gets four tries for each turn.

2. Birthday Cake
   Child puts the correct number of candles on a cake.

MATERIALS

- cake pan or round circle (8")
- number stencils
- sticker dots
- bears

CONSTRUCTION

Use a round circle pattern or cake pan. Put a large numeral in the middle and the match-ing number of dots around the outside edge. Bears can be candles.

3. Bears In and Out
4. Patterning— child's choice or Color Bear Patterning
5. Bingo— Milton Bradley Game
6. sort by color
7. multiply; count by 2 s, count by 3 s
8. simple addition facts
9. outline number shapes (4 – 6")
10. outline letter patterns (4 – 6")
11. free exploration
12. more— less
13. create a story
14. weight on balance scale

Texture Bears

Child matches bears which "feel" the same. (Activity may be done with a blindfold).

MATERIALS

- assorted "feely" materials: sandpaper, felt, velvet, cork, fur, foil, corrugated cardboard, etc.
- posterboard
- markers
- glue
- blindfold (optional)
- scissors

CONSTRUCTION

Trace two bears on posterboard for each available material. Cut out bears. Glue the "feely" materials to the bears. Cut out. Make sure edges of "feely" materials are securely glued.

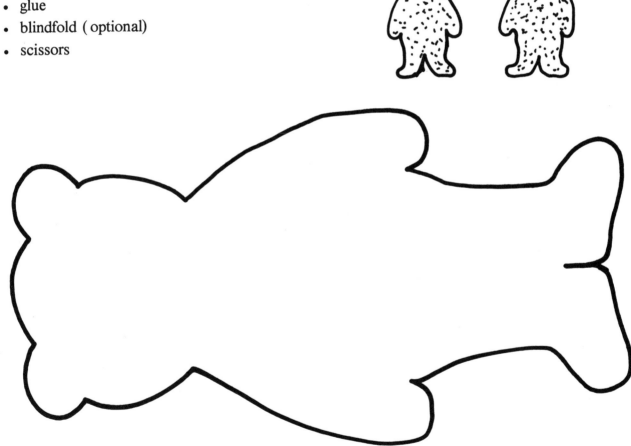

Texture Bears

147

Three Bears' House

Child practices house number.

MATERIALS
* copies of *Three Bears' House*
* tagboard or posterboard
* markers
* Laminator or Contact paper

CONSTRUCTION
Reproduce copies of *Three Bears' House* on tagboard (or traced and mounted on posterboard). Color if desired. Laminate or Contact.

PLAY
Child writes house number in the space provided. Teacher provides a model as appropriate.
Variation:
1. Each child is given a duplicated copy to complete and take home.
2. Child writes name on lines provided.

Chapter Five

MOTOR ACTIVITIES

CENTER ACTIVITIES
FOR MOTOR SKILLS

This chapter includes activities which develop gross and fine motor skills. Specific art activities are included in this chapter to help develop fine motor skills.

GROSS AND FINE MOTOR ACTIVITIES

Bean Bag Bear

Bear Tracks

Fashion Bear

Lace a Bear

Movement Cubes

Rock-a-Bear

FINE MOTOR PRACTICE PAGES

Dot to Dot

Numbered Dot to Dot

Go to Bed

Honey Path

Maze One: Going Home

Maze Two: Find the Honey

ART TASK CARDS

Circle Bear

Circle Teddy Bear

Finger Print Bears

Three Bears House Task Card

Bean Bag Bear

Child handles the beanbag in a controlled manner.

MATERIALS

- brown and tan felt or brown doubleknit fabric
- black permanent marker
- bear pattern or alternate— DANCING FELT PUPPET (Chapter 3)
- soybeans or navy beans (approximately 1½ cup)

CONSTRUCTION

Trace and cut two bears from fabric. Add features to one side using felt or marker. Stitch the two layers of fabric together leaving a small opening for filling. Fill with beans and stitch opening closed.

PLAY VARIATIONS

1. Reasonable personal choice
2. Catch with a friend
3. Toss in a basket
4. Balance bean bag on head
5. Use with BEAR TRACKS
   a. Toss BEAN BAG to specific color
   b. Toss BEAN BAG to specific letter

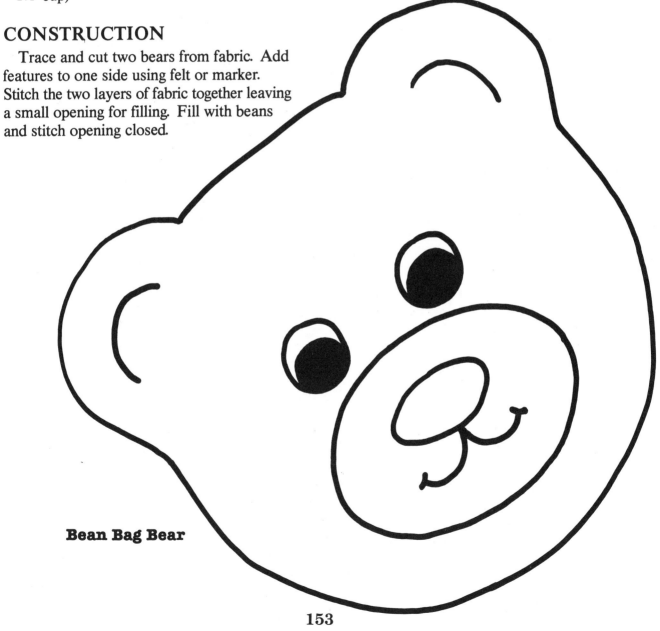

Bean Bag Bear

Bear Tracks

Child walks or follows the tracks.

MATERIALS

- Teddy Bear footprint (track) or stencil
- blank 4" x 6" index cards or oaktag (about 50) (option: rubber stair treads or foam-back carpet)
- marker, black wide tip
- Laminator or Contact paper

CONSTRUCTION

Duplicate or copy track on cards. (It is not necessary to cut them out). Go over outline
with marker if copy isn't dark enough. Laminate or cover with Contact paper as desired.

Option 1: Add letters, colors or shapes to tracks, the Laminate or Contact.

Option 2: Cut exact footprint out of rubber or carpet.

PLAY

Child follows tracks around room.
Variations:

1. Place tracks in walking pattern. Child is directed to walk forward/backward or a certain number of steps.
2. Place tracks in random pattern around room on tables, under tables, etc. Direct child to walk or crawl on tracks "over," "under," "on," "around."
3. Place tracks in walking pattern, varying distance between them to improve balancing skills. Tracks may require child to turn corners.
4. Use Option #1 tracks with colors, letters or number, place tracks around room. Child is required to identify items while walking.
5. Use Option #1 tracks, direct child to step on tracks identified by teacher or another child.
6. Place tracks in a walking pattern. Child is given a basket and asked to follow the tracks, and pick up items along the path and place them in the basket without letting feet leave the tracks.

Bear Tracks

154

Fashion Bear

Child dresses and undresses a bear.

MATERIALS
- Teddy Bear (16 – 20")
- assortment of infant clothes with buttons, snaps, zippers, ties, etc. (It may be necessary for buttons and button holes to be made larger than normal infant clothes.)

PLAY
Child practices the skills necessary to manipulate clothes fasteners. Child can practice spontaneously or follow directions of another, or prepare the bear family for an outing.

Lace A Bear

Child laces bear figure.

MATERIALS
- tagboard or posterboard
- markers
- paper drill or punch
- shoestring
- Laminator or Contact paper

CONSTRUCTION
1. Trace bear figure onto posterboard.
2. Laminate or cover with Contact paper.
3. Punch lacing holes around edge of bear. Edge of holes may have to be re-sealed using a (not too hot) tacking iron on laminated bear. Protect the film by covering with white paper. If Contacted, press hole edges down with fingers or cold iron.
4. Secure shoestring by tying knot in one end or taping one end to the back of the figure.

Lace a Bear

Movement Cubes

Child imitates movement shown on cube.

MATERIALS

- four half-gallon milk cartons
- black permanent marker
- bear picture patterns if desired
- numeral patterns 1 – 6
- white Contact paper

CONSTRUCTION (for two cubes)

Cut off milk cartons so they are as tall as they are wide. Make a cube by fitting the open end of one carton inside the other. Cover the cube with white Contact paper.

On the first cube, put one numeral (1 – 6) on each side. On the second cube, trace a bear action picture on each of the sides. (Or cut out pictures and mount on cube and cover with clear Contact paper). Pictures may be labeled: toe touch, seat spin, knee bend, jumping jack, hop and jump.

PLAY

The cubes are rolled. Child (or class) performs the action shown the appropriate number of times.

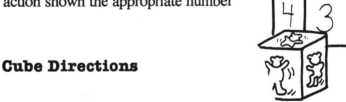

Cube Directions

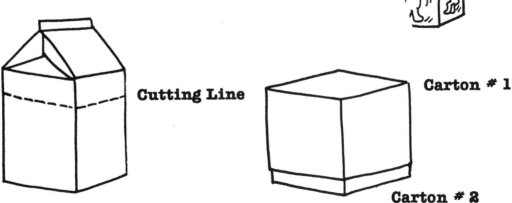

Cutting Line   **Carton # 1**

Carton # 2

157

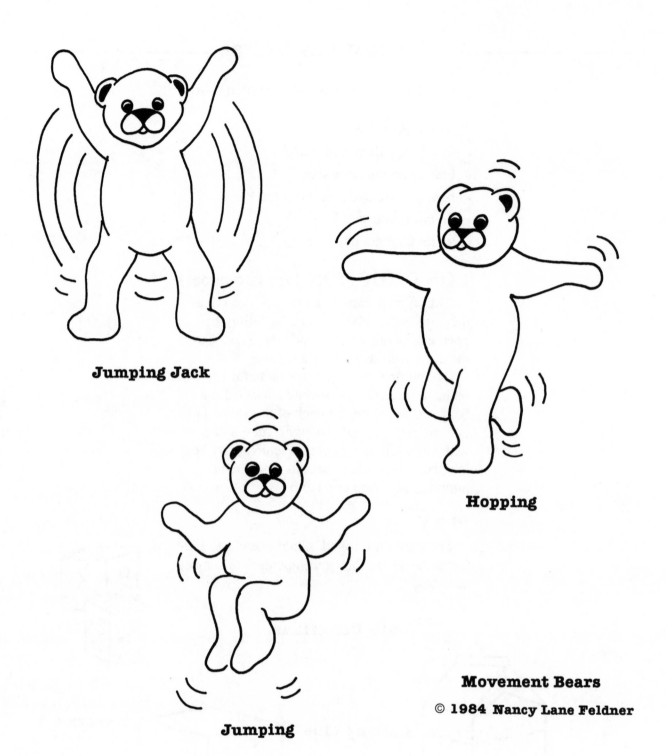

Jumping Jack

Hopping

Jumping

Movement Bears

© 1984 Nancy Lane Feldner

Knee Bends

Sit Spin

Toe Touch

© 1984 Nancy Lane Feldner

159

Rock-A-Bear

Child works with another to move bear using towel.

MATERIALS
- Teddy Bear for each pair
- bath towel for each pair

PLAY
Children face each other in pairs. Each child holds two corners at the end of the towel. Teddy Bear is placed on the towel. Children work together to swing the bear smoothly.

Variation: Pairs swing the bear, then work together to pass the bear from their towel to the towel of another pair of children.

FINE MOTOR PRACTICE PAGES

Dot to Dot

Numbered Dot to Dot

Go to Bed

Honey Path

Maze One: Going Home

Maze Two: Find the Honey

Child completes path or line.

MATERIALS
- white oak tag (9" x 12")
- fine motor practice pages
- markers

CONSTRUCTION
Reproduce pattern page on tag. Decorate with markers as desired. (Note: Many commercial copy machines can produce on tag.) Contact or Laminate.

Optional Construction: Duplicate pattern page on paper for each child.

Honey Path— Special Instructions: Sample is shown with three styles of path lines. If additional path variations are desired, remove lines on one copy, run copies with no lines and add different path lines.

Dot to Dot

161

Numbered Dot to Dot

162

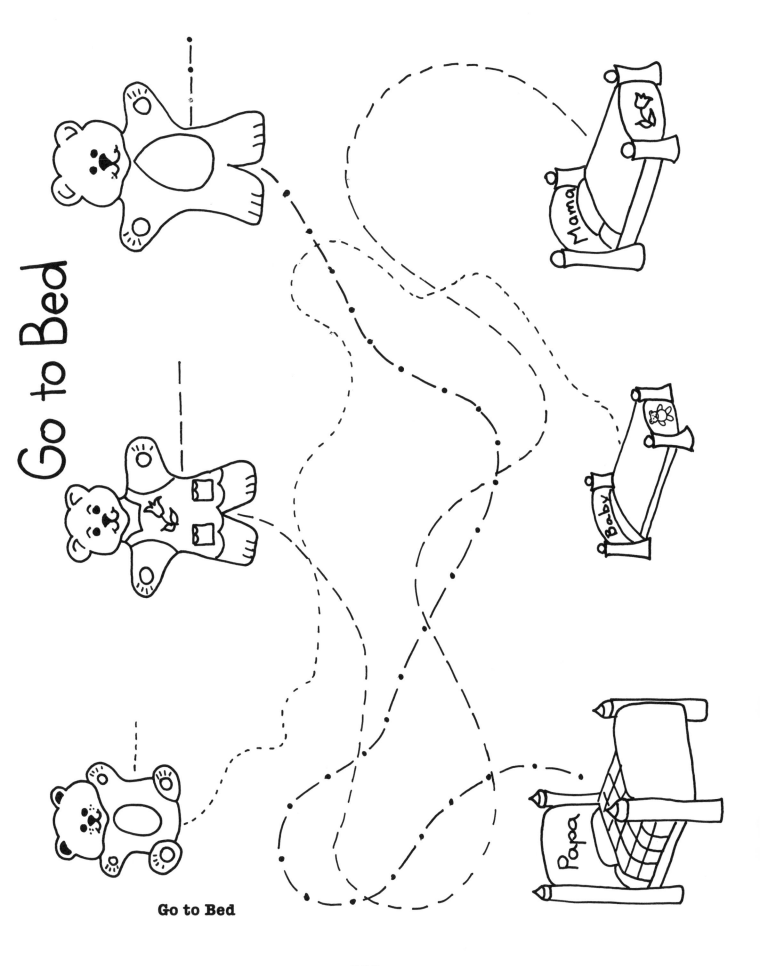

Go to Bed

Go to Bed

Honey Path

desired, remove lines on one copy, run copies with no lines, and add different path lines.

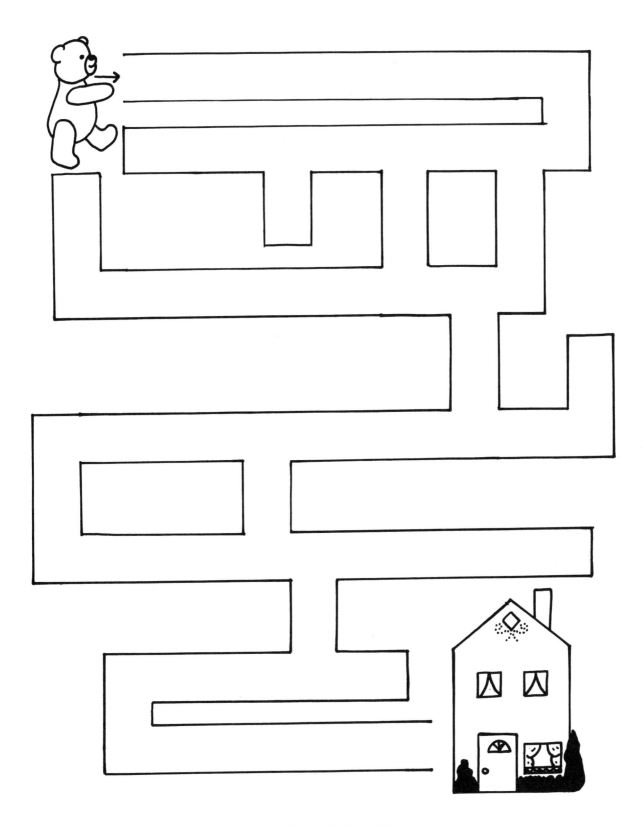

Maze 1 — Going Home

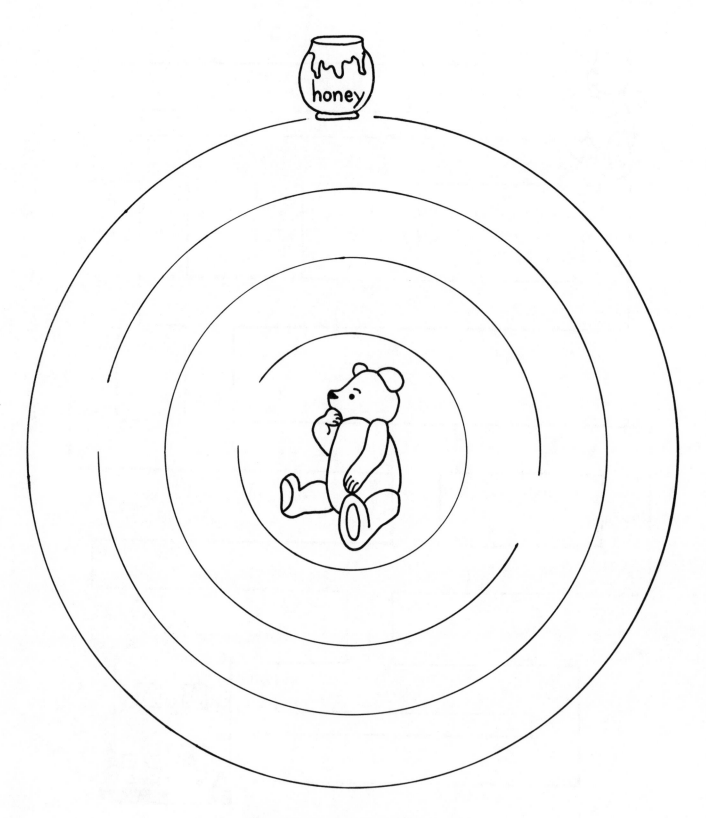

Maze 2 — Find the Honey

Circle Bear

Circle Teddy Bear

Finger Print Bear

Three Bears' House

Child completes project following task card directions.

CONSTRUCTION

(See TASK CARD DEVELOPMENT, Chapter 2)

Reproduce task cards on tag. Contact or laminate.

MATERIALS NEEDED
FOR CENTER PROJECTS

1. Circle Bear
   - TASK CARD
   - paper (12" x 18")
   - crayons
   - circle patterns or circle templates (approximately 2½", 3", 4", 6")

2. Circle Teddy Bear
   - TASK CARD
   - brown construction paper (12" x 18")
   - crayons
   - scissors
   - glue or paste
   - pencil
   - circle patterns or circle templates (approximately 2½", 3", 4", 6")

3. Finger Print Bear
   - TASK CARD
   - small piece of paper (4" x 6")
   - ink pad or stamp pad
   - fine line markers

4. Three Bears' House (page XX??)
   - TASK CARD
   - paper (12" x 18")
   - scissors
   - crayons

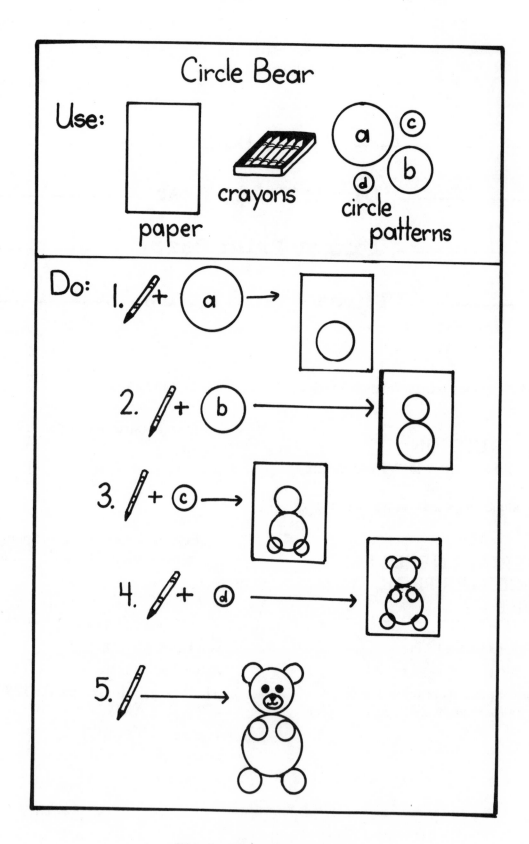

Circle Bear

Use: paper crayons circle patterns

a c b d

Do: 1. ✏ + a →
2. ✏ + b →
3. ✏ + c →
4. ✏ + d →
5. ✏ →

Circle Bear Task Card

168

Circle Teddy Bear

Use: pencil   scissors   Glue   crayons

brown paper

circle patterns   a   b   c   d

Do:
1. pencil + trace →

2. scissors + cut →

3. Glue + →

4. pencil →

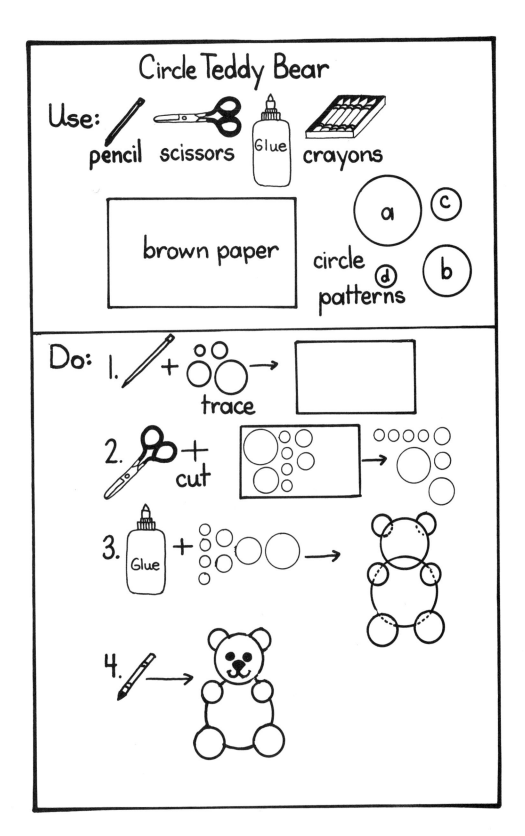

Circle Teddy Bear Task Card

169

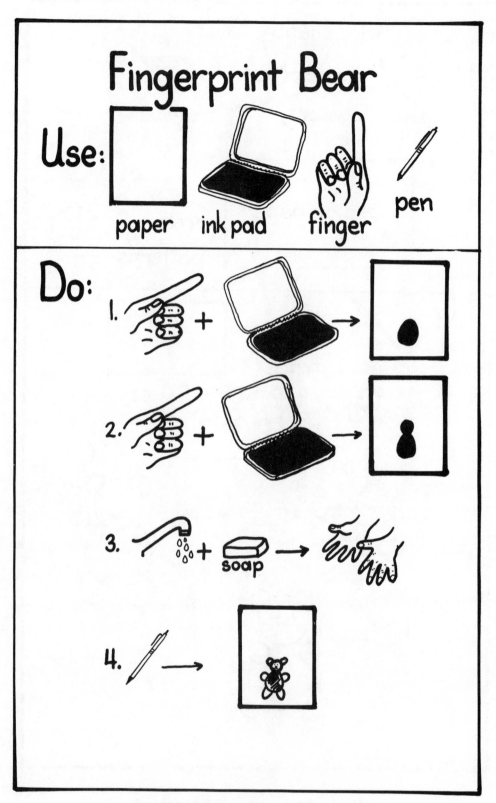

Fingerprint Bear

Use: paper   ink pad   finger   pen

Do:
1.
2.
3. soap
4.

Finger Print Bear Task Card

170

Three Bears House

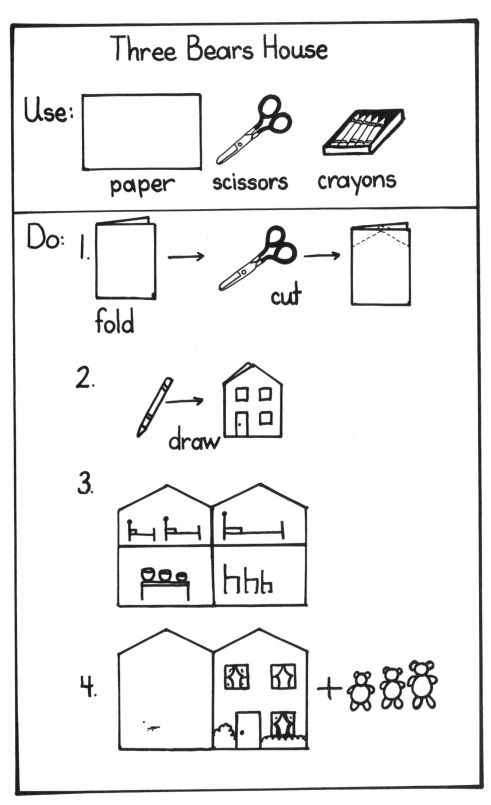

Use: paper   scissors   crayons

Do: 1. fold   cut

2. draw

3.

4. +

Three Bears' House Task Card

Chapter Six

TEDDY BEAR ACTIVITIES IN A SELF- CONCEPT UNIT

TEDDY BEAR ACTIVITIES
IN A SELF-CONCEPT UNIT

Young children learn best individually and in small groups, as shown in the Teddy Bear Center. However, in school, it is at times necessary to teach larger groups. The Teddy Bear Unit was developed to show how individual academic activities, such as writing numbers, can meet Self-Concept objectives. In addition to the center activities, Teacher directed activities are also described.

Self-concept is each child's view of himself (or herself). At school, the self concept is affected by the way children relate to others, the success they have in school, and the understanding they have of themselves. At school, a healthy teacher-pupil relationship is most important. In addition, there are things which can be done to help each child improve self-concept. The Teddy Bear is the continuing theme as activities for each category are identified.

Body Awareness	Homes
Clothing	Personal Facts
Familiar Happenings	Possessions
Family	Problem Solving
Feelings	Senses
Food	Tasks Assuring Success
Friends	

Note: the games to meet self-concept objectives for this chapter are cross referenced to other chapters.

SELF-CONCEPT UNIT

I. Body Awareness
    A. Each child identifies and describes body parts.
        *1. Graphing Bears Characteristics (page 187)
        *2. Bear Words (page 50)
        *3. Peanut Butter Play Dough (page 189)
        *4. Recycle a Bear (page 102)
         5. Sequence Bears (page 143)
         6. Finger Print Bear (page 170)
         7. Bear Body Puzzle (page 49)
         8. Body Word Puzzle (page 53)

    B. Each child will explore different ways to move.
        *1. Did You Ever See a Teddy Bear? (page 193)
        *2. Teddy Bear Dance (page 193)
        *3. Teddy Bear Says (page 193)
         4. Bear on a Chair (page 50)
         5. Bear Tracks (page 154)
         6. Movement Cubes (page 157)
         7. Puppet Pages (pages 82–96)

II. Clothing
    A. Each child names and describes articles of clothing.
        *1. Graphing Bear Characteristics (page 187)
        *2. Read Watanabe's *How Do I Put It On?* (page 118)
         3. Dress a Bear (page 59)
         4. Bear Twins (page 123)
         5. Texture Bears (page 147)

    B. Each child selects appropriate clothing.
        1. Weather Bear (page 61)
        2. Sequence Bears (page 143)

    C. Each child works with clothing fasteners.
        1. Lace a Bear (page 155)
        2. Fashion Bear (page 155)

III. Familiar Happenings
    A. Each child retells a familiar story.
        *1. Dramatization (pages 82–106)
        *2. Three Part Story (page 185)
         3. Storyteller (page 75)
         4. Story Box (page 74)

* **denotes group activities**

175

B. Each Child will describe familiar things.
    1. Bear Bag (page 48)
  *2. What's in the Pocket (page 103)
    3. Shopping With Mama (page 74)
    4. Bear Words (page 50)

IV. Family
A. Each identifies immediate family members.
    1. Matrix (page 138)
    2. Felt Story (page 102)
B. Each child identifies roles of the family members.
    1. Dramatization of The Three Bears (pages 98–100)
  *2. Family Roles (page 104)
  *3. Family Roles Discussion (page 102)

V. Feelings
A. Each child identifies and tells about feelings.
  *1. Retell a Story (page 103)
  *2. Willy's Fears (page 103)
  *3. Things We Fear (page 103)
  *4. Coping (page 102)
  *5. Feelings (page 183)
B. Each child demonstrates a feeling.
    1. Hug a Bear (page 62)
  *2. Precious Pocket (page 103)
  *3. Dramatization of The Three Bears (pages 98–100)

VI. Food
A. Each child identifies and describes common and favorite foods.
    1. Shopping with Mama (page 74)
  *2. Cinnamon Bear (page 188)
B. Each child plans and prepares food.
  *1. Finger Jello (page 190)
    2. Picnic (page 69)

VII. Friends
A. Each child tells on characteristic of friends.
  *1. Retell a Story (Ways With a Good Book, Chapter 3)
    *a. *Ira Sleeps Over* (page 106)
    *b. *The Lazy Bear* (page 106)
    *c. *Corduroy* (page 102)
    *d. *Pocket for Corduroy* (page 103)
    2. Characteristics
    *a. Comparing Friends (page 103)
    *b. Security (page 106)
    *c. Bear Words (page 50)

B. Each child cooperatively plays a game.

VIII. Homes

A. Each child gives his address.
1. Three Bears' House (page 148)
2. Teddy Bear Counters (page 146)

B. Each child describes and classifies furniture.
1. Matrix (page 138)
2. Go To Bed (page 163)

C. Each child describes and compares different types of homes.
1. Retell Story: *Corduroy* (page 102)
*2. Compare versions of The Three Bears (page 98)
3. Felt Story
a. *Theodore* (page 104)
b. *Good as New* (page 102)

IX. Personal Facts

A. Each child practices his or her name.
1. Write a Bear (Name) (page 81)
2. Teddy Bear Counters (page 146)
3. Letter Sweater (page 63)

B. Each child practices his address.
1. Three Bears' House (page 148)
2. Teddy Bear Counters (page 146)

C. Each child practices his phone number.
1. Write a Bear (Number) (page 81)
2. Teddy Bear Counters (page 146)

D. Each child tells or shows his age.
1. Teddy Bear Counters (page 146)
2. Birthday Cake (page 146)

X. Possessions

A. Each child names a favorite or important possession.
1. Touch and Tell (page 79)
2. Shopping With Mama (page 74)
*3. Security (page 106)

B. Each child describes favorite or important possessions.
*1. Introductions (page 181)
*2. Precious Pocket (page 103)

XI. Problem Solving

A. Each child recognizes and describes a problem.
1. Draw Traps (page 101)
2. Retell *Bear Hunt* (page 101)
*3. Three Part Story (page 185)

B. Each child helps solve a problem.
    1. Alter Original Story (pages 98–100)
    2. Puppet Pages (pages 82–96)
    3. Story Box (page 74)

XII. Senses
  A. Identify the five senses.
    *1. Cinnamon Bears (page 188)
  B. Using the five senses.
    1. Hearing
      a. Echo Bear (page 128)
      b. Bear on a Chair (page 50)
      c. Teddy Bear Music (page 193)
    2. Tasting
      *a. Peanut Butter Playdough (page 189)
      *b. Finger Jello (page 190)
      *c. Biscuits and Honey (page 189)
      *d. Ginger Bears (page 190)
    3. Smell
      a. Belly Button Bears (page 124)
      *b. Food Experiences (pages 188–90)
    4. Touch
      a. Texture Bears (page 147)
      b. Touch Fabrics (page 102)
      c. Touch and Tell (page 79)
    5. Sight
      a. Matching Games (pages 120, 123, 124, 130, 138, 143, 147)
      *b. Graphing Bear Characteristics (page 187)

XIII. Tasks Assuring Success
  A. Each child will complete one task on paper.
    1. Circle Bear (page 168)
    *2. Teddy Bears on Parade (page 192)
    3. Mazes (pages 165–66)
    4. Dot To Dot (page 161)
    5. Go To Bed (page 163)

  B. Each child will complete one verbal task.
    1. Touch and Tell (page 79)
    *2. Feelings (page 183)
    3. Storyteller (page 75)

Happy
Bear Day

Chapter Seven

TEDDY BEAR DAY AND OTHER GROUP ACTIVITIES

Teddy Bears are invited to be our special guests on Teddy Bear Day Thursday, October 27, If no bears live at your house, borrowed bears or stuffed animals are welcome.

GROUP ACTIVITIES WHICH EXTEND THE TEDDY BEAR CENTER

The emphasis of *Teddy Bears at School* has been the use of the center approach in working with young children and to the development of the center. The total program and the center are mutually supportive and each adds to the interest and effectiveness of the other. The group activities in this chapter are in these categories:

Teddy Bear Day   Food Experiences

Language Experience   Teddy Bear Art Projects

Adapting Familiar Activities and Games

Teddy Bear Day

Teddy Bears are invited to school on Teddy Bear Day. In addition to participating in the Teddy Bear Center, they are invited to participate in many other bear related activities including:

Language
  Invitations
  Name Tags
  Introductions
  Bear Words
Social Studies
  Tour
Mathematics
  Graphing
  Dismissal

Art
  Teddy Bear Parade
Snack
  Peanut Butter Play Dough
Physical Education and Music
  Movement Cubes
  Teddy Bear Dance
  Did You Ever See a Teddy?
  Teddy Bear, Teddy Bear, Turn Around
Literature
  Three Bears

1. INVITATIONS
Each child contributes ideas to a group invitation.
Procedure: After a discussion about Teddy Bear day, the teacher records the information the children want on the invitation. Copies are reproduced. Each child may draw a bear on his copy of the invitation. (See the illustration). The invitation is a reminder about the correct date, and reassures the parent that this is a special occasion when the children are allowed to bring a toy to school. Although most of the children will be able to bring a bear from home, the teacher should provide some extras.

2. NAME TAGS
Each child names his bear.
Procedure: Child tells teacher the name of the bear. The teacher writes the bear's name on the name tag and adds the child's last name.

3. INTRODUCTIONS
Each child introduces and describes his bear.
Procedure: The children are seated in a circle. Each child is encouraged to answer the following questions:
  How old is your bear?
  How did you choose your bear's name?
  What special things can your bear do?
  If your bear could talk, how would his voice sound?
  What do you and your bear like to do together?

4. BEAR WORDS
Child dictates specific bear words for the teacher to record.
Procedure: See *Bear Words* activity.

5. TOUR
Child identifies different areas and significant adults in the school.
Procedure: Children and bears go visiting around the school. (principal, custodian, offices, cafeteria).

181

6. GRAPHING BEAR CHARACTERISTICS

Child classifies bears by one or more criteria.

Procedure: Child contributes to group discussion and bear graph. (See *Graphing Bears* activity).

7. DISMISSAL

Child classifies bear by one or more criteria.

Procedure: Children are dismissed for the day according to type or color of bear.

8. TEDDY BEAR PARADE

Child creates bear pictures.

Procedure: Child draws bear portrait for parade mural. (See *Teddy Bear Parade* activity).

9. PEANUT BUTTER PLAY DOUGH

Child forms balls.

Procedure: Child forms bear with Peanut Butter Play Dough and samples snack. (See *Peanut Butter Play Dough* activity).

10. MOVEMENT CUBES

Child participates in group movement activities.

Procedure: Child responds to directions on cubes. (See *Movement Cubes* activity).

11. TEDDY BEAR MUSIC AND DANCE

Child responds to the directions in music.

Procedure: Child responds to record and/or imitates leader. (See *Teddy Bear Dance, Did You Ever See a Teddy?, Teddy Bear, Teddy Bear, Turn Around* activities).

12. THE THREE BEARS

Child listens and retells the story.

Procedure: See *Literature, Ways With a Good Book* activities.

Language is a part of every phase of a child's life. In addition to the center activities, quality books are a valuable tool in developing language. (See the Chapter on Literature). Large group activities such as the following also have a place in the Early Childhood Program.

Feelings   Three Part Story
Class Sequence Books   Graphing

1. FEELINGS

Child dictates sentence describing feelings (emotions).

MATERIALS

- 12" x 18" white construction paper
- colored construction paper, five pieces (3" x 5") of different colors per child
- scissors
- glue
- black marker
- one set of bear faces per child (see following illustrations)
- crayons (optional)

PROCEDURE

1. Reproduce one set of bear faces per child.
2. Cut out one set of five balloons so each child may choose the five he likes.
3. Glue one set of the five bear faces along the 18" bottom edge.
4. Working individually, teacher asks the child to finish the following statements. Write each statement on a balloon.

    I feel happy when. . .
    I feeel sad when. . .
    I feel surprised when. . .
    I feel angry when. . .
    I feel afraid when. . .

5. Glue each balloon above the appropriate bear face, connecting the balloon and the bear with a line indicating a balloon string.
6. Child may choose to color the bears.
7. DO NOT DISPLAY THESE ON THE BULLETIN BOARD. Some of the comments may be very personal.

happy

angry

scared

sad

surprised

Expression Bears
© 1984
Nancy Lane Feldner

184

2. THREE PART STORY
Child dictates story and draws pictures.

MATERIALS
- pencil
- crayons
- story picture paper, folded or (12" x 18")
- paper, lined across the bottom

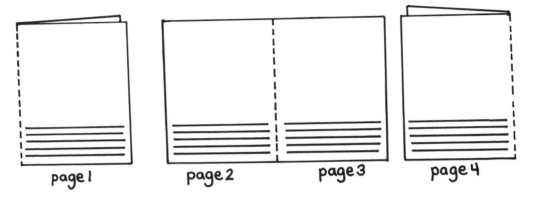

page 1   page 2   page 3   page 4

PROCEDURE

Page 1. Title. Teacher discusses possible topics with child. Child chooses topic that is very easy to draw (stick figure, Teddy Bear face). Child draws and names central character. Teacher records character name (now title) and child's name.

Page 2. Setting. Child discusses with teacher and identifies additional character and/ or setting and draws. Child and teacher condense discussion to one sentence and teacher records.

Page 3. Problem. Child discusses possible plots with teacher. Child selects plot and draws. Child and teacher condense plot to one or two sentences and teacher records.

Page 4. Solution. Child discusses possible solution with teacher. Child chooses solution and draws. Child and teacher condense solution to one or two sentences and records.

Variation: Writing a three part story can be a very enjoyable small group activity—especially if all five children are writing about the same main character. After a group discussion in which each of the five children choose a name and draw their main character on the title page, the teacher could write all five titles and authors' names during the discussion. Then all could proceed to the second page. Following this practice, possible story lines could be:

- Benjamin Bear
- Benjamin Bear lives on a shelf with other toys.
- He was lost.
- We found Benjamin in a tree.

- Blue Bear
- Blue Bear is sad. Blue has no friends.
- Sally found a bear friend for Blue.
- Blue Bear and Red Bear play all day.

3. CLASS SEQUENCE BOOK

Each child contributes to the planning and creating a sequence story.

MATERIALS

- marker
- 9" x 12" white construction paper (one for each participant)

PROCEDURE

A Class Sequence Book is best planned after a very significant time in the lives of the students. It is necessary to have a strong desire to retell experience in sequence. One reason to make a Sequence Book is because the class has really enjoyed a literature book. After reading it several times, produce your own version. A second reason to make a book is to describe a field trip to another class or Open House. It must be a "special time" or a "special book." There must be much class enthusiasm.

1. Before the class discussion begins, teacher needs to outline the experience, making sure that enough possibilities exist for different drawings by each student.
2. Discuss the total experience, encouraging children to describe in detail the part they liked the best.
3. As good verbal pictures develop, the teacher and the class should summarize. The teacher then records the idea in one or two sentences per page.
4. When the class enthusiasm has dwindled, the teacher needs to ask leading questions such as:
   "What was the name of . . . ?"
   "Which was larger, the one that Tommy saw or yours?"
   "I remember something very large and red. It was behind the cashier. What was that?"
   "What did you like the best?"
   "After we looked at the antique bears, what was the name of the next tall white bear?"

5. Remember to include supportive experiences in which the class participated:
   - Our Trip to the Toy Store (title page)
   - Authors' names
   - We wrote a letter to the toy store manager
   - Mr. Smith wrote us a letter to tell us the date and time.
   - We drew a map to the toy store.
   - We went on a school bus to the shopping center.
   - First we saw the miniature toys in the window.
   - Mr. Smith gave us a catalog.
   - We each held a Steiff bear.
   - Clark's mom took our picture.
   - We got on the school bus and came home.
6. After you cooperatively have agreed on sentences so that enough possibilities exist, the teacher needs to record those sentences at the bottom of the picture. Children need to choose the picture they want to draw. A few suggestions:
   a. The children need to understand that their picture must go with the words that are on the page.
   b. Give your least able children their first choice of pictures to draw.
   c. When you have about five remaining pages (and hopefully your five most cooperative artists), explain to them that these five pages need to be completed, review all five and allow them to discuss which child should draw which picture. At times it might be necessary to have two children complete on of these pictures (one child draws the antique bear, one draws the store manager).
7. When each child has completed his drawing to go with the assigned sentence have the children decide the order for the pictures.

186

a. It might be appropriate to do this by displaying the pictures one at a time, and then determining where each additional picture should go— before, between, after, etc.

b. This could be done as children sit in a circle with pictures under their chins.

c. Perhaps it might be best to post your "book" on a long bulletin board so that all can enjoy.

8. Eventually, staple your pages together, with the cover so the children can "read" their book.

4. GRAPHING BEARS

Child participates in the development of a bar graph.

MATERIALS

- graph paper with one- inch squares or one- inch lined chart paper (add vertical lines)
- crayons
- catalog pictures of Teddy Bears of different colors or small bear pictures colored to represent the different bear colors.

CONSTRUCTION

Glue small pictures across the bottom of the paper. Skip one vertical column between each of the bears.

PROCEDURE

Each child, in turn, will choose a crayon which approximates the color of his Teddy Bear. He will color in one space in the column above the appropriate bear. The group will then determine the most frequent color, least frequent, etc..

Variation: Similar bar graphs may be developed according to other classification criteria such as:

- long fur / short fur
- musical / non- musical / growler
- one color / multi- color
- big / little / medium size
- type of eyes
- type of nose
- jointed / non- jointed
- dressed / not dressed

Food Experiences

Preparing and serving food in the classroom offers the children the opportunity to develop language, mathematics, and fine motor skills. It offers the chance to taste new and different foods and practice good manners.

Cinnamon Bears
Peanut Butter Playdough
Biscuits and Honey
Ginger Bears
Finger Jello

1. CINNAMON BEARS

Each child participates in a sensory experience.

MATERIALS

- lined chart paper or writing paper
- marker
- Cinnamon Bears or other edibles with a variety of characteristics

PROCEDURE

Divide the chart paper (or their writing paper) into six parts. Boxes may be labeled: (draw around) bear, see, hear, feel, smell, taste. Have children close their eyes. Distribute bears. Instruct children to feel, smell, listen, and look. DO NOT EAT YET! Encourage many responses and supportive opinions for each box. Experimentation should be encouraged.

- Can you see through the bear?
- Does it feel slippery to you?
- What's another word that means sugary?
- Tap it on your desk. Lick it and see.
- Does it feel the same on your teeth as in your hand?

The finished product might look like this:

Hear	Taste
plop tap squish	red hot cinnamon too sweet good bad

See	Smell
red bumpy bear	cinnamon hot

Cinnamon Bear	Feel
	smooth chewy sugar

2. PEANUT BUTTER PLAYDOUGH BEAR

Child models a bear using no-bake cookie dough.

MATERIALS

- task card recipe
- equipment
    bowl
    measuring cup
    spoon
    wax paper
- ingredients:
    peanut butter
    honey
    powdered milk
    rolled oats (optional)

PEANUT BUTTER PLAYDOUGH (No-Bake Cookies)

Mix in a large bowl:
    1 cup of peanut butter
    ½ cup of honey
    1½ cups powdered milk
    (Optional) 1 cup of rolled oats
    (uncooked quick)
    ½ cup of honey
If dough is too dry, add honey, if it is too sticky, add milk.

PROCEDURE

Follow directions on the task card to make playdough. Give each child wax paper and a two-inch ball of dough (approx. ¼ cup). Encourage each child to model the dough to form a Teddy Bear. Demonstrations of modeling techniques (rolling small balls, make a "rope") may be given by the teacher if needed, but the child should be allowed to create his own Teddy Bear.

Variations:
1. Modeling clay.
2. Salt Ceramic Dough.
    1 cup salt
    1 cup flour (or more)
    1 Tablespoon of Alum
    a few drops of oil
    water to appropriate consistency
    may be colored with tempera or food coloring
3. Other modeling compounds of your choice.

3. BISCUITS AND HONEY

Each child writes honey B on a biscuit.

MATERIALS

- biscuits
- honey in a squirt bottle

PROCEDURE

Each child uses a squirt bottle to put honey on his biscuit during snack time.

4. GINGER BEARS

Each child makes a ginger bear.

MATERIALS

- school mixer
- spatula
- measuring cup
- measuring spoons
- waxed paper
- decorations (optional)
    raisins
    red hots
    any cookie decorations
    tube icing to write name

Recipe for 25 Bears   (Temperature 350°)

15 cups of flour
1¼ cups sugar
4 cups of molasses
5 eggs
1⅔ cup salad oil
5 teaspoons ginger
5 teaspoons cinnamon
5 tablespoons baking powder

Mix dough using school mixer. Separate into two inch balls. Chill.

PROCEDURE

Distribute squares of wax paper. Distribute dough. Form bears. Decorate before baking. Place tiny name tags under bears before baking. (Bears change in appearance in the oven). Using tube icing, initial bears after baking.

5. FINGER JELLO (KNOX BLOX)

Each child forms bears using finger jello.

MATERIALS

- measuring cup
- bowl
- spoon
- boiling water
- 9" x 13" pan
- flavored gelatin
- unflavored gelatin

RECIPE

4 envelopes of unflavored gelatin
3 three-ounce packages of flavored gelatin
4 cups of boiling water

Dissolve gelatin in a 9" x 13" pan. (Yield: 100 one-inch squares).

PROCEDURE

Make gelatin before class. Use circle cookie cutter or small Teddy Bear metal cookie cutter to form bears.

Variation: Make b using jello squares.

Teddy Bear Art Projects

The presence of the Teddy Bears and bear items in the room may motivate the children to experiment with a variety of art media. Each child feels free to explore because the wide variety of bears makes his own version acceptable.

1. COFFEE TEDDY
Child creates Teddy using coffee grounds.

MATERIALS
- 12" x 18" manila or colored construction paper
- crayons
- diluted glue (⅓ water, ⅔ glue)
- easel brush (½")
- coffee grounds, used, dried
- tray

PROCEDURE

Child draws Circle Teddy or another original bear. Child paints bear with diluted glue, trying not to get glue on facial features. Child sprinkles dried coffee grounds over the bear and shakes off excess grounds into tray. Let dry. Child scrapes off any grounds which cover eyes, noses and mouth area.

2. TEDDY BEAR QUILT
Child draws Teddy Bear for class quilt.

MATERIALS
- 9" x 9" white construction paper for each child
- 9" x 9" yellow construction paper for each child
- Laminator (optional)

PROCEDURE

Child draws and colors Teddy Bear on white paper. Quilt Construction. Laminate if desired. Tape yellow squares to white bear squares alternating colors. (Squares may be mounted on 36" mural paper if desired). A good size quilt for 20 students would contain eight rows, five squares each. To even up rows, have some children make more bears or add yellow squares. Use as wall hanging or bulletin board decoration.

3. TEDDY BEARS ON PARADE
Child draws bear for mural.

MATERIALS
- 9" x 12" manila paper
- crayons
- scissors
- 18" roll paper (yellow or white)

PLAY

Child draws and colors a picture of his Teddy Bear. Depending on the level of scissors skills, either child or teacher cuts out the bear. Attach bears to 18" roll paper. Write each bear's name under the bear.

4. TEDDY BEAR PENNANT
Child creates a personal Teddy Bear flag.
MATERIALS
- yellow construction paper (9" x 12")
- crayons
- balloon sticks
- scissors
- tape (transparent)
- Teddy Bear stickers or rubber stamps (optional)

CONSTRUCTION
Cut yellow paper into triangles about 7" x 12". At wide end of the flag (triangle), child can draw and color a Teddy Bear. Depending upon the skill level, either child or teacher writes "Happy Bear Day" on the flag. Child may draw additional bears or bear faces on the flag (or may rubber stamp small bears or place bear stickers). Pennant is attached to the balloon stick with tape. Pennant may stand at the child's desk by mounting the balloon stick in a one-inch cube of modeling clay. Pennant may be carried as child participates in "Teddy Bear Parade".

5. WALK IN THE WOODS MURAL
Child constructs appropriate part of class mural.
MATERIALS
- construction paper scraps
- mural background paper
- scissors
- glue or paste
- crayons/paint

PROCEDURE
After class discussion about *The Three Bears*, and its many versions, children suggest what might be seen on a walk in the woods. Children volunteer for responsibility for key parts and help with the background including trees, animals and flowers.

6. CLASS BOOK
Child draws a page for class book.
MATERIALS
- one page for each child
- crayons
- book covers, heavy paper on oak tag
- Laminator or Contact paper

PROCEDURE
Books are usually a culminating activity for a topic the children know well. The teacher may suggest a topic such as:
- My Favorite Bear
- The Three Bears Take a Trip
- Bear Catalog
- Things a Bear May Want to Buy
- Costumes for a Bear

It is helpful if the book is planned before anyone starts to draw. During a class discussion, ideas for pages can be recorded, and children volunteer for a page. A sentence or labels can be put on the page, with the child's help, before, during or after the drawing. One student can draw the cover. All children may be listed as illustrators. Laminate or Contact the cover.

Shape books are also very interesting to do. Choose a bear such as Lace a Bear. Duplicate one page for each child. The paper may be lined for writers or children may draw on paper one thing a bear might like.

Adapting Familiar Activities And Games

Many of the traditional games and activities used in Early Childhood Programs can be easily adapted to complement a center theme. Group games do not often take place within a center because of space requirements and the number of children involved. A selection of games is included because many of them assist in developing skills and concepts in the motor and language areas. They also promote better social skills.

Teddy Bears Says (Simon Says)
Did You Ever See a Teddy…?
(… Lassie)
Bears Are Loose (Upset the Fruit Basket)
Teddy Bear Relay

Blueberry Pass
Busy Bear
Blanket Toss
Teddy Bear Hunt (Bear Hunt)
Teddy Bear, Teddy Bear, Turn Around

When seeking activities, do not overlook the rich supply already available such as the recordings of:

Teddy Bears' Picnic
Me and My Teddy Bear

Teddy Bear Dance
The Bear Went Over the Mountain

1. TEDDY BEAR SAYS
Child follows direction of leader.

PROCEDURE

Traditional Game (Simon Says) with children performing only those actions preceded by "Teddy Bear says." Play can be vigorous, including jumping jacks and knee bends; or very subdued, touch ears, or wiggling nose.

2. DID YOU EVER SEE A TEDDY . . . ?
Child follows movement of another to a familiar song.

PROCEDURE

Variation of a familiar song, "Did you ever see a Lassie?" Using the same melody with one word change, children stand in a circle singing, one child in the center. Center child performs a movement pattern (hopping, jumping, clapping, etc.); the other children imitate that movement. Choose a new child to be IT and continue.

3. BEARS ARE LOOSE
(Variation of Upset the Fruit Basket) Child moves across circle as directed.

PROCEDURE

Children sit on chairs in a circle. Depending on the number of children in the group, choose four or five famous bear names. (e.g., Teddy, Paddington, Pooh Bear, Corduroy, Theodore). Teacher goes around the circle giving a bear name to each child. Four or five children will have the same name. One child is chosen to be first in the center; his chair is removed from the circle so that there is one more child than chairs for the game. Center child calls out the name of one bear. All children having that bear name must change chairs while the center child also tries to get a chair.

The child now without a chair becomes the center child who will call out a bear name. If center child chooses, he may call "Bears are loose!" This requires all the children to change chairs. (Children will probably need to be reminded to be careful of each other — the game tends to become extremely exciting!) If possible, continue play until all children have a turn in the center.

4. TEDDY BEAR RELAY
Child participates in a relay.

PROCEDURE

Divide students into equal teams. Line up one behind the other. The first student in the line holds a Teddy Bear. At the signal, the bears are passed back over the head to the next student and on back the line. When the last child receives the bear, he runs to the front and starts the bear back through the line again. Winning team is the one to get the original first child back to the head of the line first.

Variation: Pass the bear back between the legs.

5. BUSY BEAR
Child follows directions and touches body of partner.

PROCEDURE

Children are paired off. Leader gives directions such as, "Partners touch shoulders, Partners touch heads.," etc. Partners must touch each other with the body part named — shoulder to shoulder, head to head, back to back. Emphasis should be placed on the lesser known body parts (e. g. wrist, ankle, elbow, heel, palm, calf, thigh). Periodically, the leader calls, "Busy Bears!" When this call is heard, everyone gets a new partner.

6. BLANKET TOSS
Child works with other children to move Teddy Bears with blanket.

MATERIALS
• lightweight blanket or small parachute
• Teddy Bear

PROCEDURE

A group of children hold the blanket around the edges. Teddy Bear is placed in the center and children work together to flip the blanket up and down to bounce the Bear.

7. TEDDY BEAR HUNT
Child participates in a group activity.

PROCEDURE

This is a variation of a traditional activity long enjoyed by young children. Feel free to alter the story to fit the experiences of your children. Substitute names of local streets, rivers, toy stores, etc. Children follow the leader's actions.

STORY:

I really need your help today! This morning when I got to school, I discovered that our Teddy Bear was missing. I know that no one would take him away. He must have decided to go exploring. Let's go on a Teddy Bear hunt and see if we can find him.

Let's put on our coats, button them all the way down. It rained last night so the ground is wet. We'd better put on our boots. Don't forget your hat. Are you all ready? Here we go!

Let's go on a Teddy Bear hunt. (Clap hands on thighs like footsteps.) Go through the room, open the door, (motion) close the door. Here we go down the hall and outside. Maybe Teddy went up the hill. Let's go up. Oh! This is a steep hill. (Slow clapping).

I . . . . don't know . . . . if I can . . . make it . . . all the way . . . to the . . . . top. There. We did it! Now let's run down the other side. (Clap hands on thighs as fast as possible).

Does anyone see our Teddy Bear? No? Let's look over by the pond. Oh, look at this "ooey-gooey mud." It's a good thing we wore our boots today! (Make squishing sound by cupping hands and hitting the heels of hands together).

Maybe if we climb this tree we will be able to see Teddy. (Climbing motion). Let's look to the right. Now look to the left. Oh dear— no bear yet. Let's go down the tree. Hold on tight.

Do you suppose Teddy Bear went down to the Shopping Center to visit the other bears at the Toy Store? Let's cross the field and go see. My, this grass is tall. Stay close behind me. (Brush hands together to make swishing sound).

Now we have to cross the road. Remember to stop and look both ways. OK. Let's walk across the street. Keep watching for cars.

Here's another field with high grass. Stay close. (Swishing sound). Oh! I forgot about the river. Let's swim across. Oh! It's cold. (Shiver) (Or, find a boat and row across singing, "Row, Row, Row Your Boat.")

Here we are at the edge of the Shopping Center. Let's go to the Toy Store. Just look at all the different toys. Does anyone see Teddy yet? Maybe we'd better tiptoe back to the animal section so we don't frighten them.

Oh, look! Up there on the top shelf— there he is — sound asleep with his friends. Let's reach up and get him. Careful now— we don't want to wake him up. Tuck him inside your coat.

Oh, dear! It's almost time for you to go home. We'd better get back to school as fast as we can go!

Go back the way you came, as fast as you can, doing all the motions in reverse.

Open the door. Shut the door. Whew! Back at last. Teddy's awake. Give him a big hug!

8. TEDDY BEAR, TEDDY BEAR, TURN AROUND

Child says verse and participates in the action.

PROCEDURE

Children follow the teacher's lead in saying the verse and performing the appropriate actions.

VARIATIONS:

1. Say it happily.
2. Say it sadly.
3. Say it loudly.
4. Say is sleepily.

Teddy Bear, Teddy Bear, Turn Around

Teddy Bear, Teddy Bear, turn around.
  (Turn around).
Teddy Bear, Teddy Bear, touch the ground.
  (Touch ground).
Teddy Bear, Teddy Bear, how do you do?
  (Shake hands with neighbor).
Teddy Bear, Teddy Bear, I love you!
  (Bear hugs child).
Teddy Bear, Teddy Bear, go upstairs.
  (Walk in place)
Teddy Bear, Teddy Bear, say your prayers.
  (Fold hands).
Teddy Bear, Teddy Bear, turn out the light.
  (Snap out light).
Teddy Bear, Teddy Bear, say, "Goodnight!"
  (Palms together under cheek, eyes closed).
                                    – traditional

Appendix

A Brief History of The Teddy Bear

The bear was named Teddy for Theodore Roosevelt after a cartoon appeared in the *Washington Star* in November, 1902.

President Theodore Roosevelt was in Mississippi to "draw a line" to settle a border dispute with Louisiana. During an unproductive hunting expedition, Roosevelt refused to shoot a cub held by one of his aides. The cartoon by Clifford Berryman depicted Roosevelt turning his back on the cub, with the caption, "Drawing the Line in Mississippi."

There are several stories of the first Teddy Bear, two of which are very popular. One is that the *Washington Star* cartoon was seen by Morris Michtom, a New York candy store owner. His wife frequently made felt stuffed animals for display in the window. Michtom displayed the cartoon along with a felt bear labeled "Teddy's Bear." He wrote to the president for permission to use his name. Roosevelt said that he couldn't imagine what good his name would be in the stuffed-animal business, but that Mr. Michtom could use it. Today there is no documentation of the presidential letter, but the stuffed toys became so popular that the Ideal Toy Company evolved.

The other main story is from the Steiff family in Germany. Margarete Steiff made felt animals in her home in the 1880s. They became so popular her nephews joined her firm and many toys were sold at the Leipzig fair, 1893. The Steiff model bear was exhibited in Leipzig in 1903. An American store ordered 3,000 bears at that fair. One disputed story about Steiff bears indicates that bears were used as a decoration at a White House dinner. When a guest inquired as to the species, a wag replied, "Teddy."

The World Book Encyclopedia (1953 edition) describes the Koala as a small Australian animal that is also called the Teddy Bear. King Edward VII of England, took quite a liking to Koalas, and some thought that the bear was named "Ted" for him.

A Collector's Bibliography

Bialosky, Peggy and Alan. *The Teddy Bear Catalog.* Revised and Updated Edition. Workman, 1984. Prices, Care and Repair, Lore, 100s of Photos. Everything.

Bialosky, Peggy and Alan and Robert Tynes. *Making Your Own Teddy Bear.* Photographs by Jerry Darvin. Illustrated by Susan Gaber. New York: Workman, 1982. Very elaborate descriptions of how to make a bear family including many comments on material selections.

Bull, Peter., *The Teddy Bear Book.* Random, 1969, 1970. A personal story of a wide acquaintance with bears and bear people as well as a historical view of the bear.

Bull, Peter. *The Teddy Bear Book.* Winscombe, England: House of Nisbet, 1969, 1970, 1983. A beautiful collector's limited edition is an updated version of his earlier work. Bull has written a "furry, cuddly and above all, charming tribute to Teddy, who's captured the hearts of men, women and children around the world."

Bull, Peter in collaboration with Enid Irving. *A Hug of Teddy Bears.* Dutton, 1984. A richly illustrated album of old, middle-aged, and young bears from all over the world, plus a wealth of information about real and fictional bears.

Clise, Michele Durkson. *My Circle of Bears.* as told to Alf Collins. Photographs by Marsha Burns. La Jolla: Green Tiger Press, 1981. Clise / Collins present a delightfully photographed collection of bears, including elaborate personality sketches of each bear.

Conway, Shirley and Jean Wilson. *100 Years of Steiff 1880–1980.* Berlin, OH: Berlin Printing, 1980. A pictorial review of all Steiff toys produced.

DeMong, Phyllis. *Book of Celebearties & Other Bears.* Middlebury, VT: Paul S. Eriksson, Publisher, 1979. A delightful pun filled book, both bearable and unbearable.

Eaton, Seymour. *The Roosevelt Bears, Their Travels and Adventures.* illustrated by V. Floyd Campbell. NY: Dover, 1979, 1906, reprinted in full. "A good, wholesome yarn, arranged in merry jingle" was first published serially in twenty leading daily newspapers.

Hall, Carolyn Vosburg. *The Teddy Bear Craft Book, 1983.* The book includes step by step instructions for over 25 projects which include not only the traditional cuddly creatures, but also a quilt, a costume, and even a Teddy Bear chair.

Haysom, Barbara and Les Weston. *Pocket Size Teddy Bears.* Irvine, CA: Gick, 1982. Details including patterns for small bears and clothes are included. Color photographs help explain the directions.

Hutchings, Margaret. *Teddy Bears and How to Make Them.* Dover, 1964. After describing some very famous bear tales, the author gives a most detailed account of how to construct a variety of bears.

Isenberg, Barbara and Marjorie Jaffe. *Albert the Running Bear's Exercise Book.* Illustrated by Diane De Groat. NY: Clarion, 1984. A friend convinces Albert he can become a better runner by doing additional exercises. Outlines an exercise program with various levels of difficulty. (Juvenile literature).

Menton, Ted. *The World According to Hug, His First Book.* Putnam, 1984. Hug is the philosophizing Spokes Bear for the Teddy Bear craze. In delightful cartoons, Hug has an opinion on every subject. Hug is practically perfect, just ask him.

Menten, Ted. *The Teddy Bear Lover's Catalog.* NY: Deliah Communications, 1983. A unique publication with a potpourri of information including bear puzzles and prescriptions for damaged bears.

Moore, Marsha Evans. *The Teddy Bear Book.* Allen Bragdon Publishers, 153 W. 82nd Street, NY, 10024, 1984. Instructions for making traditional Teddy Bear with wardrobes and more than fifty other bear-related projects. Also includes a selection of recipes.

Moving Picture Teddies. Merrimack Publishing Co., n.d. Replica of the antique original. Child's shape story book has several sections of split pages so that children may select parts of the story.

Ober, Warren. *The Story of The Three Bears. The Evolution of an International Classic.* Delmar, NY: Scholar's Fascimiles & Reprints, 1981. Photo reproductions of fifteen versions of the tale.

Prince, Pamela. *The Secret World of Teddy Bears.* Photographs by Elaine Faris Keena. NY: Harmony, 1983. "A rare and privileged glimpse into the lives they lead when you're not there." Poems and photographs reveal what Teddy Bears do when humans aren't around.

Schoonmaker, Patricia. *A Collector's History of the Teddy Bear.* Cumberland, MD: Hobby House Press, 1981. The history of the Teddy Bear from its pre-Teddy Days down to the present time are featured in over 800 illustrations in black and white, and color. Bear related items are also featured.

Teddy Bear Journal, an Illustrated Notebook. Illustrated by Patricia Perleburg. Philadelphia: Running Press, 125 South 22nd Street, 1983. A delightful collection of soft drawings and quotations about bears.

The Teddy Bear Books. Reprinted paperback editions. Published by Merrick, 85 Fifth Avenue, NY 10003, n.d.
The Teddy Bears Come to Life
The Teddy Bears in a Smashup
The Teddy Bears on a Lark
The Teddy Bears in Hot Water

Waugh, Carol-Lynn Rossel. *Teddy Bear Artists, Romance of Making and Collecting Bears.* Cumberland, MD: Hobby House Press, 1984. This book is the perfect combination of academic research, artistic insight, bear-making tips, personal anecdotes of Teddy Bear experiences, and absolute enthusiasm for this subject matter. It is a look into the special world where Teddy Bear making is an art form.

MAGAZINES

Arctophile. Newsletter for the discerning collector of new bears. Published quarterly by "bear-in-mind," 20 Beharrel Street, Concord, MA 10742.

Bear Tracks. Published quarterly by The Good Bears of the World, Box 8236, Honolulu, Hawaii 96815.

The Teddy Bear and Friends, a Collector's Guide to Teddy Bears. Published quarterly by Hobby House Press, 900 Frederick Street, Cumberland, MD 21502.

NOTES